EXTRA VOLUME XXVIII

THE JOHNS HOPKINS STUDIES IN ROMANCE LITERATURES
AND LANGUAGES

THE THEATRE OF ANDRÉ GIDE

Evolution of a Moral Philosopher

THE THEATRE

of

ANDRÉ GIDE

Evolution of a Moral Philosopher

JAMES C. McLAREN

1971

OCTAGON BOOKS

New York

Reprinted 1971
by special arrangement with The Johns Hopkins Press

OCTAGON BOOKS
A Division of Farrar, Straus & Giroux, Inc.
19 Union Square West
New York, N. Y. 10003

Library of Congress Catalog Card Number: 73-120645

ISBN 0-374-95522-0

Manufactured by Braun-Brumfield, Inc.
Ann Arbor, Michigan

Printed in the United States of America

" Vous êtes l'enjeu, l'acteur et
le théâtre d'une grande lutte."
—from a letter of Paul Claudel to André Gide

FOREWORD

The purpose of this book is to appraise the moral evolution of André Gide through the study of a much neglected but highly significant aspect of his work: the theatre. I believe that Gide's theatre is of value, primarily, as a psychological document; that the dramatic form is ideally suited to an externalization of Gide's own moral conflict, and that the protagonists of his theatre represent, in a very real way, the participants in a constantly changing inner dialogue of moral extremes.

Chapter I stresses the subjectivity of Gide's approach to the drama and attempts to justify the consideration of his theatre as a moral and psychological document. Chapters II-VI comprise an analysis of his dramatic works and an evaluation of each play as representing the particular psychology of its author at the time of its composition. Lengthy plot summaries are restricted to the last two plays (ch. VI) where the themes and characters are totally removed from Biblical or classical sources. The concluding chapters consider Gide's plays in the light of his drama criticism and in terms of what they reveal of his over-all esthetic and moral philosophy. Notes on the stage productions of the Gide plays and a discussion of his translations and adaptations are found in the appendices. Select critical comments from the French press are included therein.

Permission to quote from their editions has been kindly granted by the Librairie Gallimard, Paris.

I would like to express here my profound debt to Professor Justin O'Brien of Columbia University. Through his lectures and seminars my interest in Gide and in the contemporary theatre gained strength and meaning, and through his encouragement and guidance this project took form. Sincere appreciation is extended to the librarians of the Fonds Rondel of the Bibliothèque de l'Arsenal in Paris for permitting access to the personal catalogues and press-clippings of the late M. Rondel; to Dr. Leo Forkey for his bibliographical suggestions; to Professors Norman Torrey, Jeanne Pleasants and Jean Hytier for their close critical reading of the original text; and, most particularily, to Professor Henry Carrington Lancaster of The Johns Hopkins University for providing the inspiration of his scholarship and the counsel of his experience.

JAMES C. MCLAREN

February, 1953

CONTENTS

ix

CONTENTS

THE THEATRE OF ANDRÉ GIDE

Evolution of a Moral Philosopher

CHAPTER I

THE PREPARATION OF THE DRAMA

1. Gide's Theatre as a Psychological Document

Predominantly literary and philosophic, the dramatic works of André Gide have never enjoyed a wide public acclaim and have, with few exceptions, been underestimated by his biographers and critics. However, this popular failure of the majority of his plays is no surprise; for Gide steadfastly refused to take anything but a subjective approach to this essentially objective *genre*; he refused to disturb the artistic value of his theatre by catering to public tastes or giving in to the exigencies of *mise en scène* and *décor*. As he writes in the *Lettres à Angèle* during the period of three of his most important plays: *Saül, Philoctète* and *Le Roi Candaule*:

> Et c'est ce qui rend la question théâtrale si passionnante; c'est que l'oeuvre dramatique est . . . 'faite pour être jouée,' pour être livrée à la foule. . . . C'est, avec toutes les prétentions qu'on voudra, une oeuvre qui ne trouve pas sa fin en elle-même, qui vit entre les acteurs et le public et qui n'existe qu'à l'aide de lui . . . Et pourtant *je ne peux considérer le drame comme soumis au public; non jamais; je le considère comme une lutte au contraire, ou mieux comme un duel contre lui—duel où le mépris du public est un des principaux éléments du triomphe.*[1]

Gide's plays exist essentially as literary documents and as revelations of their author's thought and experience. If they hold greater meaning for the reader than for the theatre-going public, it is because they are primarily philosophic and personal and avoid those esthetic and moral compromises to which plays intended for public approval must, Gide feels, be subjected. They represent the depths and complexities of their author's personality, and if their message

---

[1] *O. C.*, III, 199-200. Italics added. The abbreviation *O. C.* refers hereafter to the 15-volume Gallimard edition of Gide's *Oeuvres complètes*.

T. C. refers throughout to the 8-volume Ides et Calendes edition of Gide's *Théâtre complet*.

3

is often lost in the necessarily fast-moving, regulated pace of a stage presentation, their value to the critic and student of Gide's life and works is immense.

Perhaps nowhere—with the possible exception of the *Journal*—can one follow more closely the moral and psychological development of Gide than in his theatre—in the *mise en valeur* in each of his dramatic works of a constantly changing and evolving personality. Indeed, considered as a psychological document, the theatre would seem to have this advantage over the *Journal*: that whereas the *Journal* entries were made primarily during periods of Gide's literary inactivity and, as he himself observes, served as a revolt " contre la dislocation et l'éparpillement de la pensée . . . comme moyen d'entraînement au travail," [2]—the plays, on the other hand, represent organized works of art wherein the different phases of Gide's moral philosophy can be analyzed in a more concentrated and crystallized form. The *Journal* falls short here, for it so often seems to be more the recording of artistically unproductive events than the active and reasoned synthesis of Gide's thought at any given time.[3] Both *genres*, of course, complement each other, and the autobiographical data of the *Journal* is essential in determining the atmosphere and motivations of each play.

The predominance of the dialogue form in Gide's *récits* and *soties*, in his novel, *Les Faux-Monnayeurs*, and in much of his literary criticism, leads one to consider it as perhaps Gide's favored and most natural medium of expression. This facility in the dialogue coupled with his rejection of external pressure on art and his independent, subjective approach to the drama encourages one's view that the theatre—with its inherent dialogue form—represents the most sincere or, to use a Gidian term, ' gratuitous ' development of his thought. As he writes in 1926 :

[2] *Journal*, pp. 226-227. The single term *Journal* refers hereafter to the *Journal, 1889-1939* (Gallimard, 1948).

[3] This is true of most of the *Journal* entries written after 1900 and after the composition of his first play—the period which concerns us in this study. The opposite may be said, however, of the entries for the early 1890's (prior to *Saül*) which, as Justin O'Brien has pointed out, " are devoted almost exclusively to self-scrutiny and dreams, to philosophic hesitations and emotional unrest. . . ." (Cf. O'Brien's translation: *The Journals of André Gide*, I, vi).

Dès la première ligne de mon premier livre, j'ai cherché l'expression directe de l'état de mon personnage—telle phrase qui fût directement révélatrice de son état intérieur—plutôt que de dépeindre cet état.[4]

. . . car pour moi c'est plutôt le langage que le geste qui me renseigne.[5]

And again, in the Journal of 1941, Gide wishes he might express freely and without fear of censorship what he terms " le balancement de ma pensée ":

Elle se développerait en dialogue . . . et pousserait des branches à la fois dans des directions opposées. C'est seulement ainsi que je pourrais à peu près me satisfaire.[6]

This association of dialogue and opposition is revealed, too, in Gide's own inner dialogue of moral contrasts. He attributes this complexity, in part, to the conflict of the southern Huguenot influence, on his father's side, with the Norman Catholic tradition on his mother's side, to the fact that he was born " entre deux étoiles, fruit de deux sangs, de deux provinces et de deux confessions." [7] This duality of his nature is apparent throughout his life and works in the opposition of Puritan and pagan tendencies in his emotional life, of Biblical and Hellenic cultures in his esthetic and moral views and of classical precision and Romantic *élan* in his literary style. "*Je suis un être de dialogue*"; Gide states, "tout en moi combat et se contredit." [8] Yet this inner dialogue must be constantly maintained and balanced, he feels, for, far from being a deterrent to creative activity it is rather a sign of completeness and maturity from which the work of art can draw its depth and meaning. Such, then, is this counterbalance of sensual *élan* and Puritan restraint which, he insists, is an essential requirement for both moral and esthetic sincerity.

. . . cet *état de dialogue* qui, pour tant d'autres, est à peu près intolérable, devenait pour moi nécessaire. . . . pour moi, loin d'aboutir à la stérilité, il m'invitait au contraire à l'oeuvre d'art et précédait immédiatement la création.[9]

---

[4] *Journal des Faux-Monnayeurs, O. C.*, XIII, 52.

[5] *Ibid.*, p. 54.

[6] *Journal, 1939-1942*, p. 94.

[7] *Journal*, p. 959.

[8] *S. G. N.M., O. C.*, X, 341 note. Italics added. The abbreviation *S. G. N. M.* refers hereafter to *Si le Grain ne meurt*.

[9] " Feuillets," *Journal*, pp. 777-778.

It is in the dialogue of Gide's theatre that one can find most clearly an externalization of this inner " état de dialogue," of this dialectic of conflict wherein the fundamental extremes of his personality are in constant debate. Gide has defined each individual creation of an author as representing " une tentation différée . . . un moyen de connaissance de l'auteur sur lui-même, l'explication d'une pensée ou d'une émotion." [10] This would seem to be especially true of his own dramatic works. For in them we are provided with a view of Gide's personal psychological drama, of that inner dialogue which, as he has said, encourages and *immediately precedes* the work of art.

The following chapters will attempt to show in what way each of the plays, considered chronologically, corresponds to and synthesizes the particular psychology of its author at the time of its creation. But first, in order to understand the intensification of Gide's inner dialogue and its eventual externalization in literary form, we must consider briefly the preparation of the dramatist in the period begun by *Les Cahiers d'André Walter* (1891) and completed by *Les Nourritures terrestres* (1897).

2. Formation and Intensification of the Dialogue

Gide's works prior to the writing of *Saül* and *Philoctète* are filled with disillusion and anguish—based essentially on the domination of his personality by the strict Puritan ethic of his early education. The successive phases of narcissism and symbolism through which he passes fail to reconcile what he calls the " part de Dieu " with the " part de Satan," to rationalize the coexistence of satanic emotion and Puritanical restraint. " Je n'acceptais point de vivre sans règles," he writes in *Si le Grain ne meurt*," et les revendications de ma chair ne savaient se passer de l'assentiment de mon esprit." [11]

Gide's first published work, *Les Cahiers d'André Walter*, reflects the metaphysical, poetic dream-world of its author: " J'ai dans tout le corps et dans l'âme une inquiétude infinie. Je rêve. . . ." [12] His one wish is to escape from the illusions of the subconscious and objectivize his desires in a full and complete existence.

[10] Cf. preface to the 1929 Gallimard edition of *Le Voyage d'Urien.*
[11] *O. C.*, X, 348.
[12] *O. C.*, I, 106.

The desire for self-manifestation and the search for a practical solution to the moral problem show little progress through his association with Heredia, Mallarmé and the symbolist poets during the next few years. This period Gide refers to as " la plus obscure de ma vie . . . dont je ne me dégageai qu'à mon départ avec Paul Laurens pour l'Afrique." [13] " En ce temps je n'avais de regards que pour l'âme, de goût que pour la poésie." [14]

Le Traité du Narcisse, Le Voyage d'Urien and La Tentative amoureuse all illustrate an artist's preoccupation with a poetic, symbolic world, with the exaltation of the intellect and the subjugation of desire. Here one finds as a recurring theme the brevity and artificiality of outward forms of happiness and the importance of escaping surface illusions for the deeper truths attained through thought and meditation. " Nous rêvions en ce temps d'oeuvres d'art en dehors du temps et des contingences," he writes.[15] The world of reality is denied and the satanic side of the dialogue remains dormant and helpless before the Puritan God and the absolute but intangible values of the artist. Gide is like Luc and Rachel of the Tentative amoureuse in their search for the beauty behind the walled garden—for the truth behind the symbol: " Pour une fois ils marchèrent sans souci de la chaleur du jour, guidés par une pensée—car ce n'était plus un désir." [16]

The sensual, Dionysian side of Gide's nature finds little solace in this symbolic world of ideas and abstraction. In the esthetic approach to the moral conflict there is only deception and frustration. Such is the realization that awaits the searchers for artistic truth in the Voyage d'Urien:

> Ce voyage n'est que mon rêve,
> nous ne sommes jamais sortis
> de la chambre de nos pensées,—
> et nous avons passé la vie
> sans la voir.[17]

In October, 1893, Gide leaves for Africa and the turning point

---

[13] S. G. N. M., O. C., X, 312.

[14] Ibid., p. 317.

[15] " Lettre [inédite] à Jean Schlumberger " (mars 1935) published by Yvonne Davet, Autour des Nourritures terrestres, p. 21.

[16] O. C., I, 235.

[17] Ibid., pp. 364-365.

in his life. Here, at last, is the discovery of reality and the liberation of the emotions. Spontaneity, instinct and a joy of living replace the mirror of Narcissus and the symbol of the esthete. The inner dialogue becomes intensified and the Dionysian and Apollonian tendencies become identifiable with life.

> Cessant d'appeler tentations mes désirs, cessant d'y résister, je m'efforçai tout au contraire de les suivre. . . . satisfaire des forces; c'était à présent ma Morale. Et puis je ne voulais plus de morales; je voulais vivre puissamment. O beauté! O désirs! [18]

Yet despite this cry of revolt against morality, the fact that Satan and Ménalque have entered the dialogue to combat the Puritan conscience actually makes Gide more ' moral ' and critical than ever before.[19] Fully aware of the duality of his nature and of its constructive and destructive urges, he can now free himself from passive subjection to an imposed, a priori ethic and play an active rôle in his own development. He can now examine the moral problem psychologically and critically, in terms of his own basic conflict and experience.

> . . . car je ne pense qu'il y ait façon d'envisager la question morale et religieuse, ni de se comporter en face d'elle, qu'à certain moment de ma vie je n'aie connue et faite mienne.[20]

It is as an external expression of this new and growing moral consciousness that Gide's plays assume their full significance. Jacques Rivière once wrote of Gide's mind as " le théâtre d'un drame incessant et minutieux." [21] An analysis of Gide's plays will perhaps show that the value of his theatre lies in its externalization of this " drame incessant," in its depiction of a rich and complex personality and in the identification of its protagonists with the contrasting elements of an inner, psychological drama. From the unbalanced conflict of Saül through the humanism of Oedipe to the social concerns of Robert ou l'Intérêt général, we will trace

---

[18] Journal (oct. 1893), pp. 44-45.

[19] The esthetic sense has matured, too, with the active participation of the diabolic element in the inner dialogue, for ". . . il n'est point de véritable oeuvre d'art où n'entre la collaboration du démon."—Conférences sur Dostoïevsky, O. C., XI, 283.

[20] S. G. N. M., O. C., X, 435.

[21] Etudes, p. 205.

Gide's own evolution from a critical to a constructive moral philosophy—the gradual replacement of a mystic, Puritanical system by a more human and realistic approach.

What Gide writes in the *Journal* of his own psychological approach to the moral problem applies particularly to his dramatic works:

Le seul drame qui vraiment m'intéresse et que je voudrais toujours à nouveau relater, *c'est le débat de tout être avec ce qui l'empêche d'être authentique, avec ce qui s'oppose à son intégrité, à son intégration.* L'obstacle est le plus souvent en lui-même. Et tout le reste n'est qu'accident.[22]

And what he states as the aim of his *Retour de l'enfant prodigue* seems no less true of his theatre as a whole: ". . . je tâche à mettre en dialogue les réticences et les élans de mon esprit." [23]

---

[22] *Journal,* p. 995. Italics added.
[23] *Ibid.,* p. 237.

CHAPTER II

NARCISSISM AND GRATUITY

1. Biblical and Pagan Influences

It is not surprising that the man of dialogue and contrasts should receive his greatest inspiration, both esthetic and moral, from such contradictory sources as the Bible and the Greek myth—the one, a heritage from his early Puritan upbringing, the other an outgrowth of his humanistic studies and a natural predilection for the mysterious and the imaginative. It is in Gide's first two plays, *Saül* and *Philoctète*, written in the late 1890's and coinciding with an intensification of the inner dialogue and a new moral and critical orientation, that the coexistence and interdependence of the Biblical and Hellenic cultures seem most significant. Yet if Gide succeeds in utilizing both traditions in two well-constructed works of art, each represents, on a psychological plane, a distinct and very different side of his moral conflict.

Gide maintains throughout his life a keen intellectual interest in the Bible. However, where his approach to the Greek myth remains generally constant, his interpretation of the Scriptures is continually changing focus in reference to the particular point of integration and evolution of his own moral philosophy. The development of Gide's attitude to religion will be further clarified in reference to his later plays. It is enough to say here that at the time of writing *Saül* and *Philoctète* (1897-1898) the " part de Dieu " side of the inner dialogue is still controlled by the Old Testament God of restraint and censure, by the Jehovah of Saül. Despite the sensual liberation of the African trip, the Puritan conscience remains a strong influence and heightens the remorse and anxiety he so often feels at this period. He wishes he might act freely and independently through an inner, gratuitous urge and not always feel duty-bound to submit each act to the judgment of Puritan ethics.

10

Mes parents m'avaient habitué à agir non d'après la dictée de mon être, mais d'après une règle morale extérieure à moi et qu'ils estimaient applicable à tous les hommes. . .[1]

So it is that he opposes to the narrow, confining dogma of " une religion transmise," the pluralism and gratuity of the pagan myth. By developing and humanizing the legends of Philoctetes, Prometheus, Oedipus and Persephone, Gide shows us both an objective admiration and a deep personal longing for the independence and self-assertion of the Greek hero—for that evolution towards the " dénûment " or destitution of the ego in the face of hostility from the Gods and Fates.[2]

It must be stressed, however, that pagan gratuity, while an ideal and an urge of Gide's nature, is far from being a reality at this time. Gide would certainly seem, at this stage of his development, more closely associated with the tortured, narcissistic Saül than with the assertive, independent Philoctète. Not until some thirty years later with the play *Oedipe* can the ideal of Philoctète be considered a faithful externalization of Gide's personality. His enthusiasm for the pagan ideal in *Philoctète* must be interpreted, then, like much of his early writing, as " une gratuite expérimentation de la liberté qui lui manque." [3] The gratuitous act and individual morality of this play, while representing a goal towards which Gide is striving, should be thought of as a less faithful depiction of his true nature at that stage than the attitude of moral evaluation and self-criticism which underlies the writing of *Saül*. It is Gide's look beyond the anarchy of the " être " and the present to the joys and adventures of the " devenir "; it is an effort to offset the restraints of an imposed moral system, to counteract what Gide has called: " tout ce qu'une religion transmise avait mis autour de moi d'inutile, de trop étroit et qui limitait trop ma nature." [4]

---

[1] " Feuillets," *Journal*, p. 775.

[2] Richard Chase refers to this same cathartic function of myth in his chapter on " Myth and Psychoanalysis," *Quest for Myth*, p. 101: " I suggest that myth is the repository of repressed wishes and that part of the magic power of myth stems from its ability to furnish ' recognition scenes ' in which we have the thrilling experience of coming face to face with a disinherited part of ourselves."

[3] René Schwob, *Le Vrai Drame d'André Gide*, p. 244.

[4] *Journal*, p. 41.

Yet both Puritan restraint and pagan gratuity are essential for the proper integration of the inner dialogue. Without the extremes of an early religious formation, the wealth and diversity of Gide's works might well have been lessened; [5] but for the rigidity of his Puritan youth, he might not have introduced the pagan ethic through protest and a desire for moral harmony. As he writes in his memoirs of these two opposing tendencies:

Etrange! c'était au temps précisément de ma préparation chrétienne que cette belle ferveur païenne flambait. J'admire aujourd'hui combien peu l'un gênait l'autre.[6]

And, again, as Gide states in the *Journal*: "... je ne sais si mon admiration pour la littérature grecque et l'hellénisme n'eût pas suffi à balancer ma première formation chrétienne." [7]

At the time of writing these first plays, Gide is clearly dissatisfied with religious morality but has not yet succeeded in singling out from the dogma of church and Scriptures his later individualistic concept of Christ. While the critical approach of *Saül* shows Gide's appreciation of the Biblical principle of restraint and self-discipline, it is clear, too, from *Philoctète*, that his ideal is rather the freer and more humanistic ethic of pagan times. For, " La Grèce . . . où l'on pouvait changer de dieu sans changer pour cela de religion . . . n'a pas cherché à poser devant l'homme une sorte de canon moral. . . ." [8]

The drama of Gide and the Puritan conscience and of Saül and Jehovah is also the drama of Philoctète's struggle against the indifference of the gods. That the Greek hero emerges victorious where Saül fails, stems from his refusal to submit the inner dialogue to a single authority and from his maintenance of harmony between the psychic contrasts of his personality. For, in Gide's words: " le problème . . . c'était de maintenir l'Olympe intime en équilibre, non d'asservir et de réduire aucun des dieux." [9]

It is this very psychological significance of the Greek myth which

[5] " Evolution de ma pensée? Sans une première formation (ou déformation) chrétienne, il n'y aurait pas eu évolution du tout."—*Journal*, p. 1051.

[6] *S. G. N. M., O. C.*, X, 263.

[7] *Journal*, p. 859.

[8] *Un Esprit non prévenu*, p. 89.

[9] " Feuillets," *Journal*, p. 777.

intrigues Gide and leads him to dramatize the legends of Philoctetes, Oedipus and Persephone on a modern, humanistic plane as a sort of catalyst to his own psychological process and moral evolution. He is interested in the modernity of the Greek myth, in what ways it concerns contemporary man and provides an heroic ideal of both individualism and self-sacrifice.

Je prétends interroger la fable grecque d'une manière nouvelle, et vous dis que sa signification psychologique est intacte, que c'est cette signification-là qui nous importe et qu'il appartient à notre époque à dégager.[10]

In 1898, Gide is actually a psychological composite of elements found in both Saül and Philoctète, although he has neither sunk to the self-destructive Satanism of the one nor attained the equilibrium and self-mastery of the other. The Biblical theme, as we shall see, strikes closer to the author through its critical appraisal of already existing Gidian tendencies; the Greek theme, optimistic and constructive, represents an *élan* beyond the present towards the " devenir " and the " dénûment." [11]

In his efforts to avoid the Dionysian extremes of Saül and to realize the moral serenity and self-discipline of Philoctète, Gide will gradually approach a reconciliation of these Puritan and pagan sides of his nature. We will observe this development in discussing some of the later plays when Gide, through a final revolt against the authority of Jehovah and Puritanism, will be ready to entrust to Christ the solution of this dispute between Dionysus and Apollo.

2. *Saül* [12]

" Les Nourritures terrestres," Gide writes in the preface to the 1927 edition, " sont le livre sinon d'un malade, du moine d'un convalescent. . . . Il y a dans son lyrisme même, l'excès de celui

[10] Un Esprit non prévenu, p. 73.

[11] Freud's interpretation of the ancient peoples' respect for dreams would seem to apply to Gide's deep concern for the myth. " It is homage paid to the unsubdued and indestructible element in the human soul, to the daemonic power which furnishes the dream-wish. . . ."—The Interpretation of Dreams: Basic Writings of Sigmund Freud, p. 543.

[12] Five acts in prose, Saül was begun, July 1897, in Rome, and completed at Arco in the Tyrol early in May 1898. A fragment of the play appeared in the Revue Blanche, June 15, 1898, but the first edition was published by the Mercure de France in 1903. Saül is dedicated to the actor, Edouard de Max.

qui embrasse la vie comme quelque chose qu'il a failli perdre." [13] *Saül* represents a condemnation of the extreme sensual philosophy of the *Nourritures*.

A break with the past was a step forward for Gide, but it was impossible to rationalize permanently an ethic of hedonism.[14] The domination of the inner dialogue by the " part de Satan," Gide realizes, is as dangerous as was its earlier control by the " part de Dieu." In neither case is there any permanent elevation or spiritual growth. It is, then, through a critical appraisal of the newly-found values, that the tragedy of Saül, possessed and overcome by his demons, develops in Gide's mind.[15]

Although the general plot and characters are drawn from Book I of Samuel, there are many discrepancies between the Biblical exposition and Gide's very personal and psychological concentration on the central character.[16] The Biblical Saül, though abandoned by God, remains predominantly active and forceful to the end. Gide's character, left to his own resources, becomes pitifully passive and apathetic. In the Biblical account, it is envy of David's power and popularity that drives Saül to a relentless pursuit and persecution of his rival. With Gide, on the other hand, it is Saül's inverted affection for David that prevents him from assuming a more active, realistic rôle. Jonathan, too, in Gide's play, is no longer the courageous warrior but a helpless, almost feminine weakling. This characterization is essential, however, to the undertones of uranism throughout the play and to the general atmosphere of helplessness and despair which centres about the person of Saül and from which the tragic action springs. Gide's Jonathan, through

[13] *O. C.*, II, 227.

[14] " Car il ne me suffisait pas de m'émanciper de la règle; je prétendais légitimer mon délire, donner raison à ma folie."—*S. G. N. M.*, *O. C.*, X, 435.

[15] Gide provides a strange explanation for his choice of theme in a letter to Christian Beck, dated February 27, 1907: " C'est pour avoir trouvé dans mon jardin une chrysalide de bombyx complètement occupée par de petites chrysalides d'ichneumon que j'eus l'idée d'écrire mon *Saül* dépossédé de soi par ses démons."—" Lettres à Christian Beck," *Mercure de France*, CCCVI (août 1949), p. 619.

[16] Gide's language is particularly striking: an ordered classic prose interspersed with occasional modernisms:—" des petits crapauds " (*T. C.*, I, 13); " se piquer le nez " (p. 21); " pas tant de tapage, les petits! " (p. 60); " flanquer à la porte " (p. 108).

his obvious inability to perpetuate his father's dynasty on the throne of Israel, assumes a relatively undramatic position in the play, and allows the interplay of dialogue and dramatic tension to centre on Saül and his reactions to his antithesis, David. The secondary characters are but vague silhouettes who in no way influence the destiny of Saül and, in Jean Hytier's words, "ne sont que les prétextes d'une fatalité tragique qu'il porte en lui." [17]

What Gide has done, by way of self-criticism and self-evaluation, is to analyse the moral consequences of a sensual, undisciplined nature whose basic dialogue has been deprived of restraint and conscience. It is through the character of Saül that Gide can best investigate the relative importance of the Puritan and satanic urges in his own nature.

"Now the spirit of Jehovah departed from Saül and an evil spirit from Jehovah entered him," states Book I of Samuel. [18] Gide, starting from this point and placing emphasis on this satanic element, provides us with a pathological study of moral degeneration. But in so doing, he depicts as well the self-destruction which might readily result from an unchecked exploitation of basic tendencies in his own character.

That Satan has become a strong voice in the Gidian dialogue since the African trip is apparent from a letter to Francis Jammes at the time of the composition of this play. Gide's torments, as he describes them, closely parallel those of his protagonist, Saül.

Tous les démons de la Judée m'habitent, se nourrissent de moi, me tourmentent; si je ne les chérissais un peu, je serais beaucoup plus malheureux; mais je ne serais pas si malade. Je suis hanté. Toi . . . le plus pur de mes amis . . . et qui persistes à me croire hanté seulement par le ciel. . . . [19]

This "disposition à l'accueil," so praised by the Gide of the *Nourritures terrestres*, results in the complete suppression of Saül, his defeat by the Philistines and the loss of his kingdom. His tragic fate is not determined wholly by external events or by Providence but stems largely from within himself, from his passivity before the forces seeking the dissolution of his personality.

[17] *André Gide*, p. 209.
[18] I Samuel 16: 14.
[19] *Correspondance Gide-Jammes* (octobre 1897), p. 125.

As Gide states in a letter to one of his critics:

La dissolution de la personnalité, où menait une disposition trop passive à l'accueil, est le sujet même de mon *Saül* . . . que j'écrivis sitôt après mes *Nourritures,* en manière d'antidote et de contrepoids.[20]

Saül, abandoned by God and beset by the enemy, believes he alone can learn the secret of Israel's destiny. In contrast to the valiant and forthright David, he waits in silence and secrecy for a revelation of the future:

Je m'use à demeurer silencieux. Depuis que je me tais, mon âme se consume; comme un feu vigilant, son secret l'use jour et nuit! [21]

Throughout all this inaction and introversion, he becomes increasingly familiar with his demons whom Gide has ingeniously externalized into real beings that prance about the palace cajoling their victim and catering to his every whim.

DÉMON: Roi Saül, on a soif.
SAÜL: Oui, c'est vrai, je vais chercher la coupe.
DÉMON: Eh! non! mon bon roi! attends qu'on te l'apporte.[22]

Saül's dream-world, like that of André Walter, is one of illusion and imagination although here it is Satan and not God that prevents the integration of the individual with reality. Deprived of divine guidance, Saül is unable to exercise his own will, to balance his conflict and " passer outre," as Gide's hero Oedipe will do in a later play. " Ah! qu'est-ce que j'attends à présent pour me lever et agir! " he cries. " Ma volonté! ma volonté! . . . J'encourage tout contre moi." [23]

In the cave of the Sorceress of Endor, the ghost of the prophet Samuel speaks out against this confusion and complexity of Saül's mind:

Saül! Saül! Il est d'autres ennemis que les Philistins à soumettre; mais ce qui te meurtrit est accueilli par toi.
. . . .
. . . ce que tu nommes de la crainte, tu sais bien que c'est du désir.[24]

Saül's only consolation lies in the gratification of his demons,

---

[20] " Lettre à M. le Pasteur Ferrari " (15 mars 1928), *Lettres,* p. 532.
[21] *T. C.,* I, 96.   [23] *Ibid.,* p. 134.
[22] *Ibid.,* p. 59.   [24] *Ibid.,* p. 77.

for, "avec quoi l'homme se consolera-t-il d'une déchéance? sinon avec ce qui l'a déchu." [25] Here we have an ironic commentary on the enthusiasm of the *Nourritures* where, just two years before, Gide had written:

> Ma soif augmentait d'heure en heure, à mesure que je buvais. A la fois elle devint si véhémente que j'en aurais pleuré de désir.
>
> ....
>
> D'avoir goûté tant de bonheur, l'âme sera-t-elle jamais consolée? [26]

At the root of Saül's mental torture, however, lies his deepest, most complex secret: his sexual inversion. This theme built subtly and sometimes almost indiscernibly about the dialogues of Saül and David and of David and Jonathan, is an essentially Gidian one that has already centered in the Ménalque of the *Nourritures*, and is to be more fully treated in *L'Immoraliste, Si Le Grain ne meurt, Les Faux-Monnayeurs* and *Corydon*. Here, again, there is a parallel between Saül and the Gide of the *Cahiers* and the symbolist period. However, at the time of writing *Saül*, Gide has come to accept his sexual abnormality, despite qualms of conscience, as a basic tendency of his nature. Saül is only tortured by this problem which position and prestige prevent him from externalizing.[27] It further blinds him from reality and prevents his realization that David has been destined to succeed him on the throne. "Je voudrais tant savoir que ce n'est pas David que je dois craindre . . .," he says. "Je ne peux pas le détester! Je veux lui plaire." [28]

Saül's wearing and then discarding his beard gives symbolic strength to the eventual confession and externalization of his inverted feelings for David. At the dramatic crisis of the play, in Act III, he has the beard removed in the hope of appearing less aged and austere to the youthful David. ". . . En me vieillissant à tes yeux, elle ne pouvait pas me plaire, cette barbe royale. . . . C'est à cause de toi que je l'ai fait couper." [29] It is with somewhat

---

[25] *Ibid.*, p. 133.

[26] *O. C.*, II, 214-215.

[27] In a letter to André Rouveyre, November 22, 1924, Gide states: ". . . ce n'est pas le fait d'être uraniste qui importe, mais bien d'avoir établi sa vie, d'abord, comme si on ne l'était pas. C'est là ce qui contraint à la dissimulation, à la ruse."—*Lettres*, p. 37.

[28] *T. C.*, I, 77.

[29] *Ibid.*, p. 95.

different motives that Michel of *L'Immoraliste* shaves off his beard as a sort of wanton, unreasoned gesture to his recovery of health and strength after a long illness.[30] For Michel, as for Saül: " C'était comme si j'enlevais un masque. . . ." Michel realizes immediately, however, that his inner emotions and secret longings, previously masked, are now clearly visible for all to see: ". . . la peur venait de ce qu'il me semblait qu'on voyait à nu ma pensée et de ce que, soudain, elle me paraissait redoutable." [31] Yet Saül is too mentally ill to analyse logically the tragic repercussions of this act although subsequent developments in the play would fully justify Michel's apprehensions. Saül lacks the cunning wiles, the recourse to reason of the more sane and logical Michel. His tragic gesture but further complicates an already disintegrated mind. It prompts him to express emotions best left unsaid but which he can now no longer retain behind a veil of secrecy and convention. And so, almost in a dream, Saül pronounces to David his pitiful confession of intermingled nostalgia and desire:

SAÜL: . . . Que ne suis-je égaré dans l'ardeur du désert comme jadis, hélas! chercheur d'ânesses; dans la chaleur du jour je brûlerais! je sentirais alors moins brûlante mon âme, que le chant active, et qui s'élance, de mes lèvres, vers toi, Daoud, délicieux. (*David jette à terre la harpe qui se brise, Saül semble se réveiller*). Où suis-je? David! David! mais reste donc. . . .

DAVID: Adieu, Saül! plus pour toi seul désormais ton secret est intolérable.[32]

---

[30] It is interesting to note that Gide himself wore a beard at the time of *Saül's* composition—during that period of intense uncertainty over the application and rationalization of his new ethic. In 1902, the year of *L'Immoraliste*, the beard had been replaced by a heavy moustache. The *Journal* entries of this time indicate less secrecy and self-searching in Gide's attitude, a greater moral integration and " souci d'autrui." The moustache is finally removed in the summer of 1907 when Gide is vacationing at Jersey with Jacques Copeau and friends—this, just a few months after the completion of his *Enfant prodigue* and the formation of a new moral philosophy. Copeau refers to this " épaisse moustache tombante . . . une moustache mensongère, sauvage, intolérable. . . . C'est à Jersey . . . que nous la décrochâmes. Enfin ce grand dessinateur se dessinait sous nos yeux. Il avait trouvé sa figure. Le demi-masque était tombé, la contradiction résolue, l'erreur dissipée—" Remarques intimes en marge d'un portrait d'André Gide," *Hommage à André Gide*, p. 81.

[31] *L'Immoraliste, O. C.*, IV, 62.

[32] *T. C.*, I, 97.

Saül's complicated personality is a reflection, though an exaggerated one, of Gide's own moral conflict at this time: the antagonism of mind and body, of Apollo and Dionysus. "Ma valeur est dans ma complication," says Saül.[33] In a letter to Francis Jammes, dated August 6, 1902, Gide admits a similar struggle to reconcile his inner dialogue with reality.

Tu me sais compliqué, né d'un croisement de races, assis à un carrefour de religions, sentant en moi toutes les directions de Normands vers le sud, de Méridionaux vers le nord, portant en moi de si multiples raisons d'être, qu'une seule peut-être me demeure impossible: être simplement.[34]

Unlike Gide, however, Saül makes no effort to escape from illusion to reality, from the self to that harmony and "dénûment" for which Gide is striving. He is doomed, like Tityre in *Paludes*, to a life of inertia and moral stagnation.

Gide's moral philosophy has advanced and matured considerably here from the narcissism of André Walter, the esthetic escapism of the Symbolists and, too, from the glorification of the senses in the *Nourritures*. For Saül's tragedy lies in his exaggeration of all three ethics: his introversion, his retreat from reality and, above all, his complete subjugation to those same sensual, satanic urges so lauded by the *Nourritures*:

Nourritures!
Je m'attends à vous, nourritures.
Satisfactions! Je vous cherche.[35]

The moral lesson of this play, therefore, lies in the warning that suppression of the personality results from a destruction of that inner dialogue which, as we have seen, Gide considers the prerequisite of artistic creation and the essence of life itself. A statement in the *Journal*, many years later, strikes the key-note of Saül's problem and proposes a psychological balance between the restraint of André Walter and the self-indulgence of the *Nourritures*:

Je laisse sans violence les propositions les plus antagonistes de ma nature peu à peu s'accorder. Supprimer en soi le dialogue, c'est proprement arrêter le développement de la vie.[36]

[33] *Ibid.*, p. 132.
[34] *Correspondance Gide-Jammes*, p. 199.
[35] *O. C.*, II, 82.
[36] *Journal* (1927), p. 842.

3. *Philoctète* [37]

Gide has portrayed the misuse of individual liberty in *Saül*. He recounts its development and ultimate triumph in *Philoctète ou Le Traité des trois morales*, a humanistic and philosophic treatment of the Greek legend.

Martin-Chauffier suggests the possible influences of the Dreyfus Affair in Gide's choice of theme [38] while Richard Heyd, in his notes to the *Théâtre complet*, alludes to Gide's interest at this time in " le robinsonnisme." [39] This play, however, like all the early writings of Gide, is clearly inspired more by moral than political or social considerations. For Gide is concerned here not with the justice or injustice of Philoctète's abandonment by the Atridae but rather with the opportunities which isolation from the motivations and hypocrisies of a social milieu afford the individual for gratuitous expression and self-development.

The play forms in Gide's mind at a time when the anguish and searching of the *Journal* entries are balanced, as it were, by a fervent interest in the humanistic philosophies of Nietzsche and Dostoyevsky. In the *Lettres à Angèle*, written in 1898—the year of *Philoctète*—Gide praises Nietzsche's ethic of self-assertion and disregard for conventional moral systems. " L'horreur du repos, du confort, de tout ce qui propose à la vie une diminution, un engourdissement, un sommeil. . . ." [40]—such was Nietzsche's initial teaching with which Gide is in full accord. However, Philoctète, while illustrating this lesson through his assertion and independence, does not, at any time in the play, approach the irrational extremes of the Nietzschean superman. If Gide, like Nietzsche, has passed beyond social and religious concepts of good and evil,

---

[37] Five acts in prose, *Philoctète* was written in 1898 and first announced as *Le Traité de l'immonde blessure*. The play first appeared in the *Revue Blanche* (ler déc. 1898) and was published, in 1899, by *Mercure de France*, in a volume containing, as well, *Le Traité du Narcisse, La Tentative amoureuse* and *El Hadj*. The dedication is to Marcel Drouin (Michel Arnauld), Gide's brother-in-law and one of the founders of the *NRF*.

[38] *O. C.*, III, viii.

[39] *T. C.*, I, 184. Heyd quotes Gide's letter to Christian Beck (Dec. 21, 1907): " ' Le Robinsonnisme ' . . . m'avait tourmenté lorsque je méditais mon Philoctète." " Le Robinsonnisme " refers to the solitary existence of Defoe's Robinson Crusoe, isolated, like Philoctète, on a remote island.

[40] *O. C.*, III, 230.

beyond all uncompromising ethics imposed on the individual from without, he remains a strong exponent of a personal, self-imposed discipline. Nor does Philoctète's form of self-assertion represent the satanic, destructive individualism of Dostoyevsky's Kirillov or Raskolnikov. In all, the character of Philoctète perhaps exemplifies most completely Goethe's ideal of moderation and temperance— that concept of a rational, serviceable individualism which is gradually to replace the absolute Nietzschean ethic of Gide's earlier period of revolt and liberation. The qualities Gide ascribes to Goethe, many years later, would seem to have been already depicted, clearly and perhaps deliberately, in the characterization of Philoctète:

L'universalité même de Goethe et l'équilibre où il maintient ses facultés, ne vont pas sans une sorte de modération, de tempérance. Ou plutôt: seule la modération permet cet équilibre heureux, auquel bientôt Nietzsche se refuse. Dionysos ici triomphe. Goethe se méfie un peu de l'ivresse et préfère laisser dominer Apollon. . . . Nietzsche exigera de l'homme davantage, il est vrai; mais l'exemple de ce Titan foudroyé . . . c'est aussi bien notre fragilité qu'il remémore. A son anxieuse question: " Que peut un homme? " nul mieux que Goethe n'a répondu.[41]

Gide's hero remains logical and rational throughout, an ideal example of the correct exploitation by the individual of his resources and capabilities.

With a view to drawing attention to the moral and philosophic rather than the dramatic and pathetic possibilities of the legend, Gide has developed an economy of style [42] and plot as well as an original, humanistic approach to the characters which is far removed from the Sophoclean interpretation.[43]

[41] " Goethe," *NRF*, XXXVIII (mars 1932), p. 377.

[42] The technique of using silence rather than speech to show emotions is used frequently by Gide throughout *Philoctète*. Cf. Act I, 2; Act II, 2 and, particularly, Act 5, comprising a single two-line speech. Along with Maeterlinck (*Les Aveugles, Intérieur*) and Curel (*L'Envers d'une sainte*), he may be said, in this play, to be a precursor of the later so-called " théâtre du silence " of J. J. Bernard and Denys Amiel.

[43] Yet Gide's plot more closely resembles Sophocles' than it does the versions of Aeschylus or Euripides. The latter two introduce a chorus of Lemnian natives where Gide and Sophocles suppose Philoctetes to have been absolutely alone on the island. With Sophocles, as with Gide, Neoptolemus is the companion of Odysseus, whereas in Euripides' play,

Such incidental characters as the Sailor-Merchant are omitted
as is the chorus whose function in the Greek play of dramatizing
the sufferings of Philoctètes is quite unessential to Gide's purpose.
Sophocles' hero is overcome with hatred and self-pity. In no way
resigned to his lot, he spends his time bewailing his loneliness
and despair and his maltreatment by the Atridae. Gide's Philoctète
is a philosopher and thinker. His loneliness has taught him the
beauties of nature and virtue and the true meaning of life. With
Sophocles, it is only through the intervention of Hercules that
Philoctetes will consent to the surrender of his coveted bow and
arrow. There is no *deus ex machina* in Gide's play, no sudden
intervention of external events. Gide's hero surrenders the weapons
freely and willingly in an assertion of his freedom and independence. Ulysses, in both plays, represents the collective will of the
state, the complete devotion to the Greek cause—an attitude which
stands out all the more sharply in Gide's treatment through its
constant opposition to the devotion-to-self philosophy of Philoctète.
To Sophocles, Ulysses (Odysseus) represents *the* moral right; to
Gide, his ethic of submission before an absolute system of values
is but an *a priori* renunciation of individual liberty and moral
integrity. Gide, however, does attenuate his portrait of the calcu-
lating Greek by showing him at times to be appreciative both of
the moral qualms of Néoptolème and the heroism of Philoctète.
The nobility and sense of honor of Sophocles' Neoptolemus restrains him from conniving against Philoctetes. Gide's youth, less
adult and rational, is motivated more by instinct and emotion.
Above all, he personifies the inquiring, searching mind that Gide
so admires in the adolescent. " Mais quel est le devoir, Ulysse? "
he asks,[44] and lacking a satisfactory reply, he turns to Philoctète
with the plea: " Philoctète! enseigne-moi la vertu . . ." [45]

It is through the conflicting reactions of Néoptolème to Ulysse
and to Philoctète that the " trois morales " of the play's title
become clarified: the emotional idealism of the adolescent, the

it is Diomedes. Both Neoptolemus and Diomedes are omitted from the
Aeschylus version. (These plays of Aeschylus and Euripides are lost;
yet we know their general character from the commentaries of Dio
Chrysostomus.)

[44] *T. C.*, I, 152.

[45] *Ibid.*, p. 164.

devotion to state of the collectivist thinker and the devotion to self-betterment of the individualist. This last attitude, realized by Philoctète and representing the Gidian ideal, gains strength and purpose when considered as both the logical outgrowth of Néoptolème's quest for truth and as the direct antithesis of the authoritarian, closed ethic of Ulysse.

The psychological development of Néoptolème in this play closely parallels Gide's own search for a moral truth. Like his protagonist, Gide had been oriented early towards a rigid, inviolable ethic wherein the particular will of the individual was subordinated to the general will of the group. Like Gide's growing reaction against the cold dogma of the Puritan God, Néoptolème, too, becomes somewhat sceptical of " le mystérieux Zeus contenté " [46] who would turn even ruse and deceit to his own ends.

U: Ne crois-tu pas, Néoptolème, qu'il importe avant tout que les ordres des dieux s'accomplissent? fussent-ils accomplis sans l'aveu de chaque homme?
N: Tout ce que tu disais avant, je l'approuvais; mais à présent je ne sais plus que dire, et même il me paraît . . . [47]

In transferring his sympathies from the collectivist cause to the plight of the individual, Néoptolème is attracted not to a selfish, hedonistic form of individualism but rather to those qualities of sincerity and wisdom which Philoctète has acquired through his own efforts. Virtue, he discovers at last, is to be found more in a sincere, unmotivated expression of the individual will than in a calculated, conformist subjection to an ethic external to the self.

Gide is also aware by now that the " abandon de soi " of Philoctète rather than the " abandon à soi " of Saül and Ménalque or the absolute conformism of Ulysse stands as the most effective response of the individual to the demands of Puritan society. It is this ideal of individualism in the service of self-development, harmony and abnegation to which Gide will now devote his full efforts and which, as we have seen, has gradually replaced, in his moral philosophy, both the Puritan restraint of André Walter and the sensual abandon of the *Nourritures*.[48]

[46] *Ibid.*, p. 147.
[47] *Ibid.*, p. 153.
[48] One cannot agree with the statement of M. H. Fayer that Philoctète's individualism is: " a version of the satanic spirit which leads Dostoyevsky's

N: Mais quel est le devoir, Ulysse?
U: La voix des dieux, l'ordre de la cité, l'offrande de nous à la Grèce . . .[49]

Dissatisfied with this synonymous concept of duty and virtue, Néoptolème turns to Philoctète for an explanation. But the young man must search out the truth for himself; there is no quick and ready answer to the problem. Instead, almost as if he were testing the sincerity and earnestness of his questioner, Philoctète unfolds his secret only slowly and hesitatingly in a series of dialogues throughout the play. " Enfant! " he tells Néoptolème, " on ne parvient que pas à pas à la vertu supérieure." [50] Patience, devotion to self and self-discipline, Néoptolème gradually discovers, are the steps through which one attains this higher virtue and are the necessary attributes of " ce que l'on entreprend au-dessus de ses forces." [51] Virtue, then, is not an acquisition from the external world. It can be acquired only from within through constant devotion to the development and attainment of the self.

N: Se dévouer à quoi, Philoctète?
P: J'allais te dire: aux dieux . . . Mais c'est donc qu'au-dessus des dieux, Néoptolème, il y a quelque chose.
N: Au-dessus des dieux?
P: Oui, puisque je n'agis pas comme Ulysse.
N: Se dévouer à quoi, Philoctète? Au-dessus des dieux, qu'y a-t-il?
P: Il y a . . . soi-même.[52]

His solitude and physical suffering [53] have made of Philoctète a philosopher, have taught him the true meaning of virtue and the beauty of the sincere, disinterested act. The social being, he tells Ulysse, is incapable of performing " une action pure et vraiment désintéressée." [54] " Je m'exprime mieux depuis que je ne parle plus à des hommes. . . . Je compris que les mots sont plus

characters to self-assertion even in the sense of self-destruction."—*Gide, Freedom and Dostoyevsky*, p. 63.

[49] *T. C.*, I, 152.
[50] *Ibid.*, p. 174.
[51] *Ibid.*, p. 176.
[52] *Ibid.*, p. 169.
[53] " La maladie propose à l'homme une inquiétude nouvelle qu'il s'agit de légitimer. La valeur de Rousseau, de même que celle de Nietzsche, vient de là."—" Feuillets," *O. C.*, II, 459.
[54] *T. C.*, I, 158.

beaux dès qu'ils ne servent plus aux demandes." [55] Freed from the motivations of a social existence, he has learned to give full and spontaneous expression to his inner nature, to strive towards an even greater moral harmony and a purer esthetic appreciation. He has become " de jour en jour moins Grec, de jour en jour plus homme . . ." [56]

. . . et je voudrais mes actions de même toujours plus solides et plus belles; vraies, pures, cristallines. . . . Je voudrais parvenir à la plus grande transparence, à la suppression de mon opacité. . . . [57]

Fear of the Gods, respect for the Greek cause, consideration for Ulysse and Néoptolème: none of these normal motivations of a social being influences Philoctète to give up his sole possession to the Greeks. It is an act of pure gratuity, issuing from an inner urge for self-sacrifice, and utterly free of external cause.

It is with this " acte gratuit," [58] with this disinterested, impulsive action, that the play closes. As Ulysse and Néoptolème sail away, the sun rises in a clear blue sky and flowers appear in the snow as if to symbolize the " belle, pure, cristalline " quality of Philoctète's sacrifice. He has achieved complete harmony of his own nature and peace with the world. " Ile ne reviendront plus; ils n'ont plus d'arc à prendre . . . Je suis heureux." [59]

---

[55] *Ibid.*, pp. 160-161.

[56] *Ibid.*, p. 160.

[57] *Ibid.*, p. 163.

[58] The " acte gratuit " is further developed in *Le Prométhée mal enchaîné* (1899) where Gide's hero asserts his independence over Zeus and the ' Vulture-Conscience ': ". . . gratuit: un acte qui n'est motivé par rien . . . intérêt, passion, rien. L'acte désintéressé; né de soi . . . l'acte libre."— *O. C.*, III, 105. Gide gives an important qualification to this definition in an article, " Fait divers," *NRF*, XXX (juin 1928), p. 841: " Les mots ' acte gratuit ' sont une étiquette *provisoire* qui m'a paru commode pour désigner les actes qui échappent aux explications psychologiques . . . les gestes que ne détermine pas le simple intérêt personnel. . . . l'homme agit soit *en vue* de, et pour obtenir . . . quelque chose; soit simplement par motivation intérieure . . ."

[59] *T. C.*, I, 180.

CHAPTER III

DESIRE AND POSSESSION

1. *Le Roi Candaule* [1]

Where Greek mythology has provided Gide with an example of
integrated, serviceable individualism in the legend of Philoctetes,
it gives him a pretext for a new critical and subjective analysis
of the moral problem in the legend of Candaules, King of Lydia.
In his psychological study of the Lydian monarch, Gide is concerned again less with the narrative of events than with the study
and evaluation of essential elements of his own nature and experience. The illusory, intellectual world of André Walter and the
Symbolists, the tendency towards risk and irrationalism of the
Nietzschean period and the evangelical fervor of the *Nourritures*:
all these Gidian tendencies motivate Candaule and lead to his
downfall.

Although Gide's preface alludes only to the *Clio* of Herodotus,
the basic plot of his play owes much, as well, to that version of the
legend found in the *Republic* of Plato. The stress on psychology
and character development, however, owes little to the Greeks.
Indeed, one would be justified in singling out *Le Roi Candaule* as
an outstanding example of Gide's reinterpretation of the Greek
myth and in indulging, at this point, in a very brief comparison
of Gide's play with three other significant treatments—two classic
and one modern—of the same theme.

Herodotus introduces Gyges as a member of the King's body-
guard whom Candaules specially favoured. However, his social
background and the poverty of his earlier existence are not stressed

[1] This play, comprising three acts in verse-form, was written during the
summer of 1899 and first published in the Sept., Nov. and Dec. issues of
L'Ermitage. The original edition, with author's preface, was published
by the *Revue Blanche* in 1901. The dedication is to Georges Rondeaux,
brother of Mme André Gide.

as they are in the Gide play. The Queen is not mentioned by name and there is no recourse, on the part of Gyges, to a magic ring with powers of invisibility. The Gyges of the Greek historian is prompted by Candaules to observe the Queen in her bed-chamber but he does not seduce her as in Gide's treatment. The Queen then provokes Gyges to murder the King as punishment for his betrayal and disrespect. Gyges subsequently marries the Queen and the justification of his act is established through confirmation by the Delphic oracle of his accession to the throne. Herodotus does not insist on any moral interpretation of the legend but does hint at that trait of irrational generosity in Candaules which is to be the core of Gide's characterization: " All affairs of greatest moment were entrusted by Candaules to this person, and to him he was wont to extoll the surpassing beauty of his wife." [2]

Plato's version of the legend has, not surprisingly, a distinctly moralistic flavor.[3] The magic ring of Gide's play is introduced by Plato as responsible for awakening the criminal instinct in Gyges. While exploring a cavern laid bare by an earthquake, Gyges, a shepherd in the King's service, discovers the ring on the finger of a dead man entombed within a hollow, brazen horse. Armed with the invisible charms of the ring, he proceeds to court, seduces the Queen, kills the King and takes over the throne. No mention is made of the Queen's collusion in the crime and the victim, Candaules, is mentioned but once and then not by name.

The aim of Gide, unlike his Greek models, is clearly to centre the entire moral responsibility for events on Candaule and to relegate Gygès and Nyssia to secondary rôles. This he does by analyzing the problem of possession through knowledge, of that emotional reliance on reactions external to the self that Herodotus has suggested but left undeveloped. The fact that Gygès is a fisherman in Gide's play adds striking irony to the discovery of the magic ring inside a fish served at the court banquet. The ring

---

[2] *History of Herodotus* (tr. by George Rawlingson), I, 151.

[3] Cf. Platon, *Oeuvres complètes* (Collection Budé), paras. 359-360.

Plato's moral lesson on the evil effects of the ring is found again in Cicero, *De Officiis* III, para. 38.

Yet another non-dramatic treatment of the legend with which Gide was doubtless familiar is Théophile Gautier's *nouvelle*, *Le Roi Candaule*. Gide likely got the name " Nyssia " from this source.

passes directly into the King's possession and responsibility, and it is he who, in turn, imparts its secret to the pauper Gygès, thereby opening his own world of abstract thought and illusion to the passions and realities of human nature.

A brief word of comparison between Gide's play and that of Friedrich Hebbel: *Gyges und sein Ring* (1856) seems pertinent here, again with a view to bringing out the originality and psychological insight of Gide's theatre. Gide himself is aware, in 1905, of an " intéressant parallèle " between the two works,[4] one which is more sharply defined by the German critics less than three years later (Jan. 8, 1908) when *Le Roi Candaule* was given an unenthusiastic reception by Berlin audiences and, naturally enough, was compared unfavorably to the better known play of Hebbel. Certainly, Hebbel's is the more suitable for dramatic staging and public comprehension. It is terse, deliberate and unphilosophic where Gide's play is obscure and psychological, confined, both in theme and presentation, more to the realm of thought than action.

In the Hebbel play, it is Gyges, warrior-courtier of the King, who makes a gift of the ring to Kandaules. The dramatic action springs, as with Gide, from the King's desire to make others aware of his wealth. However, Hebbel does not attempt to analyse this state of mind. It is a less deepset and determining factor here than with Gide's hero and simply provides that important 'single error' which prepares the *dénouement* and the drastic atonement at the play's end.

> I want some soul to witness that I'm not
> A futile fool, a mere self-dupe that boasts
> He has the fairest woman for his kissing.
> I fill the want with you.[5]

Having provided Gyges with the magic ring, Kandaules persuades him to view the naked charms of the Queen, Rhodope. The

[4] *Journal*, p. 176.

Modern treatments of *Le Roi Candaule*, though in a lighter, less serious vein, include that of Michel Carré and that of Meilhac and Halévy, presented in Paris in 1865 and 1873, respectively. *Le Roi Candaule* of Maurice Donnay was produced in 1920 at the Opéra-Comique.

[5] *Three Plays of Friedrich Hebbel: Gyges und sein Ring* (tr. by L. H. Allen), p. 19.

latter subsequently urges Gyges to avenge her honor by murdering the King, but Gyges will consent only to a fair and open combat with his friend. The reluctant adversaries agree that Rhodope will be the victor's prize and the combat ensues with both maintaining their honesty and decorum throughout and Gyges finally emerging from the fray to claim the Queen. Rhodope, of course, remains true to her promise and proceeds to the altar with Gyges to complete the vows of marriage. This contract fulfilled, Rhodope stabs herself in a final act of virtue and self-sacrifice.

> My stain is purged
> For none has seen me save for whom 'twas meet.
> But now I disunite myself from you.[6]

It can be seen from this short synopsis that Hebbel's characters, apart from the single error of Kandaules, are essentially virtuous, well-meaning and unselfishly devoted both to one another and to a higher ideal of honor and integrity. The 'error' of Gide's Candaule has much deeper psychological roots as has the treachery of the Queen and the transformation of Gygès from a somewhat ingenuous *nouveau riche* to murderer and usurper. For all three have deep within them dormant urges which need but the pressure of time and events to be unleashed. The poverty and hardships of Gygès' early life (a factor stressed only in Gide's treatment) break out in the form of confusion and passion before the luxuries and temptations of the court. Nyssia, long resigned to the passive, unsympathetic status of a 'possession' of the King, appears cunning and forceful when the occasion permits. And finally, Candaule, himself, discovers too late that he is the victim of those very flesh-and-blood persons whom he had thought to be but the slaves and puppets of his illusory world and through whom he had sought a symbolic realization of his own powers.

Gide is aware in the preface to *Le Roi Candaule* of the " étrangeté de cette pièce et le malentendu qu'elle risquerait d'amener." [7] The misunderstanding and controversy have arisen largely over what many critics believe to be the political intentions of the work. Charles Maurras had seen in *Candaule* " des allusions politiques profondes." [8] Raymond Lepoutre, while admitting the

[6] *Ibid.*, p. 66.   [7] *T. C.*, II, 29.
[8] Quoted by Gide in his " Préface à la seconde édition," *T. C.*, II, 40.

irrationalism and selfishness of Candaule's acts, sees in his deep-felt need for sharing his possessions a preview of Gide's later interest in communism.[9] And Robert Kemp, a drama critic of our own day, sees in the unveiled Nyssia a symbol of universal suffrage. Candaule's error, he feels, can be considered in a political light as " celle des détenteurs du pouvoir qui le livrent imprudem-ment à la masse."[10] In an attempt to prove that Gide was not ' converted ' to communism in 1932 but was politically and idealogi-cally pro-communist as early as 1899, Jean Louverné insists on the political significance of *Le Roi Candaule*. It was, he argues, rather the King than the husband of Nyssia whom Gygès murdered in a calculated revolt against subjection and authority.

Il exécute un capitaliste dont il a entrevu l'existence criminelle. Ce ' meurtre ' d'un membre des ' classes dirigeantes,' je veux le considérer comme un symbole dramatique de la lutte des classes; peut-être, aussi, comme un exemple.[11]

Writing in the *Nouvelle Revue Française* in reply to the argu-ments of Louverné, Albert Thibaudet sees little grounds for insisting on Gide's political intentions in this work. Thibaudet recalls Gide's preface concerning the origins of the play and his reference to a certain article which had urged that exhibitions of beauty—specifically, the public display of a beautiful nude woman —be made available by the " classes dirigeantes " for the enlighten-ment of the masses. The mysterious author of this article, Thibaudet reveals, was none other than Gide's close friend, Pierre Loüys. " Le ' peuple ' abstrait de Loüys . . . il l'a appelé Gygès, il a appelé les classes dirigeantes Candaule. *Le Roi Candaule* fait partie d'un dialogue avec Pierre Loüys." [12] Gide's " pente rapide " towards communism in the 1930 's was not, then, in evidence at the time of his writing *Le Roi Candaule*. Indeed, the exact opposite of Louverné's thesis might as readily be made by interpreting the play as a sympathetic warning to conservatives and aristocrats to hold firm against the greedy incursions of the lower classes. " *Le Roi Candaule* serait un mythe sans pente," concludes Thibaudet,

[9] Raymond Lepoutre, *André Gide* (1946), pp. 80-83.

[10] Robert Kemp, *Lectures dramatiques* (1947), p. 246.

[11] " Conversion?," *NRF*, XLII (avril 1934), p. 635.

[12] " Conversions et Conclusions," *NRF*, XLII (juin 1934), p. 1001.

"du temps où Gide en effet était sans pente, ou n'avait qu'une pente modérée." [13]

"Question sociale?—certes," Gide writes in 1897. "Mais la question morale est antécédente." [14] And, it is important to note, the moral problem continues to dominate the social in Gide's writings until after 1918 when a greater harmony and integration of his personality will promote a more objective interest in social and political issues. In 1899, however, at the time of *Candaule*, Gide remains primarily concerned with moral and esthetic questions. He is still searching for a workable ethic and still depicting and criticizing the basic tendencies of his own nature through the protagonists of his plays and *récits*. *Le Roi Candaule* is no exception. Gide's investigations on the moral plane remain perfectly compatible with the work of art for they are totally subjective and in no way represent an objective, utilitarian attitude on the author's part. "La part d'idées," he writes in the preface to *Candaule*, "... doit rester ... au service de la beauté." [15] Political and social theses must remain outside the domain of art. His lecture in Brussels in 1904, for example, decries the all too prevalent utilitarianism of the theatre. The dramatic work, he believes, should be "une oeuvre délibérément et manifestement artistique." [16] As late as 1910, Gide has strong criticism for the political stress of Jean-Marc Bernard's writings in *Les Guêpes*. "Sans doute la politique nous presse aujourd'hui d'une manière très urgente," he states, "mais la politique se développe sur un plan, la littérature sur un autre." [17] And again, as he writes of the anticlerical theme of Jules Renard's *La Bigote*: "L'oeuvre d'art *ne doit rien prouver*; ne peut rien prouver sans tricherie." [18]

It seems abundantly clear, then, that Gide's purpose in *Le Roi Candaule* is not to uphold the lower classes against the priviliged few through the opposition of Gygès and Candaule. This play does not represent a betrayal of Gide's esthetic and moral values, nor is he embarking here on a social crusade. The problem is moral

[13] *Ibid.*, p. 1003.
[14] "Réflexions. . . ." *O. C.*, II, 423.
[15] *T. C.*, II, 30.
[16] "Evolution du théâtre," *O. C.*, IV, 205.
[17] "Journal sans dates," *O. C.*, VI, 126.
[18] "Réponse à la lettre de Jules Renard," *O. C.*, VI, 135.

and psychological. The defeat of Candaule by Gygès does not symbolize the political conquest of capitalism by a communist proletariat. It represents, rather, the defeat of abstraction and illusion by reality.

In the character of Candaule, Gide condemns the romantic, irrational approach to self-fulfillment. *Philoctète* has developed the ideal of moral integration achieved independently and in isolation. *Le Roi Candaule* shows the dangers of social communication and involvement of others on the part of an unintegrated and disturbed personality—the infringement on reality of a mind that has not yet passed beyond the stage of abstract thought and illusion. Where Philoctète's abandoning of his weapons is a gratuitous act of self-sacrifice, Candaule's " générosité indécise," his display of wealth and his sacrifice of Nyssia to Gygès represent a motivated act of self-aggrandizement. Unable and unwilling to evolve from within, he seeks in the reactions and emotions of those about him a knowledge of his own worth which his possessions alone cannot provide.

" Difficulté de faire admettre une idée comme un *mobile*," Gide writes in his " Nouvelle Préface pour *Candaule*." " Non point charité—du moins pas au sens chrétien du mot: il n'y a pas là privation. . . ." [19] Lacking the necessary " dénûment " for a gratuitous affirmation of his being, Candaule is content more with the " idée," the symbol of life than with life itself.

> Mon bonheur semble
> Puiser sa force et sa violence en autrui.
> Il me semble parfois qu'il n'existe
> Que dans la connaissance qu'en ont les autres,
> Et que je ne possède
> Que lorsqu'on me sait posséder.[20]

His relations with Gygès are not determined, then, as much by sincerity and genuine friendship as by a psychological need for a verification of his own value, a knowledge he seeks not through his own merits but through the wealth at his disposal.

> GYGÈS: Roi Candaule, pourquoi tiens-tu tant
>   A ce que je connaisse ta fortune?

---

[19] " Feuillets," *O. C.*, VI, 372.
[20] *T. C.*, II, 76.

CANDAULE: Pour que te réjouisse l'amitié
Qui te fait profiter de ces biens.

GYGÈS: Je pensais que l'amitié que tu voulais
N'était pas celle de tes biens, mais de toi-même.

CANDAULE: Laisse ton ironie, Gygès,
Et ne résiste plus au bonheur.

....

Ecoute: l'inquiétude m'habitera
Tant que tu ne connaîtras pas
Dans toute sa complication, ma fortune.[21]

Edmond Jaloux has seen a homosexual leaning in Candaule's attitude to Gygès which, he believes, provides a more specific explanation of the play.[22] It seems more likely, however, that Candaule's actions have an intellectual rather than a physical or emotional basis, that his careless sacrifice of Nyssia is but a manifestation of an illusory, unrealistic approach to life—one which has a parallel in J.-J. Rousseau's idealistic conception of his relationship to Saint-Lambert and Madame d'Houdetot.[23] Such is this impractical vision of reality which Gide further clarifies many years later in an article entitled " Vérité ":

. . . car j'ai déjà remarqué combien souvent cette sorte de presbytie qu'entraîne la fixation des clartés lointaines rend indifférent ou insensible à l'aspect du monde réel. Ces âmes éblouies sont à la fois insoucieuses et incapables d'observer. Elles vivent dans une sorte de fantasmagorie mystique.[24]

Candaule's acts, therefore, stemming as they do from moral instability and illusion, contradict that ethic of gratuity and the " acte pur " which Gide had already proclaimed as early as 1894 and was later to incorporate in the character of Philoctète:

Qu'une chose, quelle qu'elle soit, ne soit point faite pour une autre chose, quelle qu'elle soit. Tout acte doit trouver sa raison d'être et sa fin en

---

[21] *Ibid.*, pp. 95-96.

[22] ". . . Candaule, au fond, aime Gygès et non Nyssia, et . . . il ne donne pas à Gygès ce qu'il a de plus précieux mais quelque chose qu'il méprise un peu, et par lequel il veut s'attacher à Gygès."—*La Revue hebdomadaire* (16 janvier 1932), p. 278.

[23] Cf. *Journal*, p. 189, for Gide's comparison of Candaule's character with aspects of Rousseau's *Confessions* and Dostoyevsky's *Idiot*.

[24] *Feuillets d'automne* (1949), p. 241.

lui-même, et ne pas être intéressé. Ne pas faire le bien ou le mal pour la récompense; l'oeuvre d'art en vue de l'action; l'amour pour de l'argent; la lutte pour la vie.[25]

Candaule's refusal to accept life other than in terms of his own vision or ideal is a problem Gide has already approached critically through the narrator of *Paludes* (1895) and will develop further in the Edouard of *Les Faux-Monnayeurs* (1926). In each case the characterization reflects that mystical, illusory aspect of Gide's nature dating from the loneliness of his Puritan youth and the idealistic abstraction of the symbolist period when the esthetic vision was sought as a solution to the moral conflict. The narrator of *Paludes* (representing, in a sense, Gide's feeling of " dissemblance " after his return from the African trip) cannot objectivize his views of reality into literary form, cannot bring himself to accept or understand the monotonous routine of those about him whose ethics do not always conform to his own intangible idea of life. He realizes, finally, that it is the selfishness of his *idea* which has led him to the same inaction and illusion as Tityre, the subject of his satire. And he cries: " Il faut qu'elle [l'idée] croisse et que je diminue." [26] Similarly, Edouard of *Les Faux-Monnayeurs* is unable to recreate in novel form those facts of reality which he has observed and noted in his *Journal*. They must be idealized and ennobled to meet his own abstract, intellectual concept of life. With Candaule, as with Narcisse, Edouard or the narrator of *Paludes*, this idealization and symbolic transformation of reality represents an evasion of moral responsibility and self-discipline. In each case, life is acceptable only in so far as it can provide a reflexion of the self, can conform to an imaginative concept of reality and thereby compensate for the inadequacy of the " moi inné."

Action and social contact must follow and not precede moral harmony, must depend on a prior realization of the self from within. Actions based on illusion and an unintegrated ethic lead only to disaster. This is the warning of Gide in *Le Roi Candaule* where not only Candaule himself but all those about him become shaken and transformed by his acts.

---

[25] " Feuillets," *Journal* (1894), p. 46.
[26] *O. C.*, I, 424.

The evangelical attitude of Candaule to Gygès, the desire to control and influence another's personality is fraught with danger, Gide realizes. This attitude, which Gide himself had assumed on his return to France after the African trip, has already been analysed in the arguments of the hero of *Paludes* with the group of *littérateurs*, in the master-disciple relationship of the narrator and Nathanaël in the *Nourritures* and in the hero of *Le Prométhée mal enchaîné* who attempts to convince his Parisian audience on the merits of the ' eagle.' Barnabé, the moralist in *Paludes*, had voiced Gide's first warning on this point in his criticism of the narrator's attitude:

Vous voulez . . . les forcer à agir sans considérer que, plus vous intervenez avant leurs actes, moins ces actes dépendent d'eux. Votre responsabilité s'en augmente; la leur en est d'autant diminuée. Or la responsabilité seule des actes fait pour chacun leur importance—et leur apparence n'est rien.[27]

The " jette mon livre " statement at the end of the *Nourritures* similarly disclaims the principle of influence and urges the disciple, Nathanaël, to make his own way in life. " Ne t'attache en toi qu'à ce que tu sens qui n'est nulle part ailleurs qu'en toi-même . . ." [28] And the drastic succession of events immediately following Gygès' conversion to Candaule's views proves even more decisively, perhaps, that Gide has by now renounced the rôle of *influenceur* for the more demanding but rewarding task of self-development and evaluation on a permanent and mature basis. " Nathanaël, j'aimerais te donner une joie que ne t'aurait donnée aucun autre . . . cette joie, je la possède," says the Gide of the *Nourritures*.[29] Yet this communication of an untried and unreliable ethic can be dangerously deceptive, Gide realizes, now that his enthusiastic *élan* has been tempered by critical judgment. For such is the tragedy of Candaule who would impart to others an idea of happiness based solely on illusion and intellectual abstraction, acquired from external sources and determined by a basic disharmony of the inner self.

PHÈDRE: Non, pas à ta richesse, Candaule,
                  Non! c'est à ton bonheur que nous buvions.

CANDAULE: Eh! c'est encore pis!
                  Qu'est-ce que vous savez de mon bonheur?

---

[27] *O. C.*, I, 413.   [28] *O. C.*, II, 223.   [29] *Ibid.*, p. 65.

> Et qu'est-ce que j'en sais moi-même?
> Est-ce qu'on peut regarder son bonheur?
> On ne voit que celui des autres;
> Le sien on ne le sent que lorsqu'on ne le regarde pas.[30]

Where the theme of abstraction and illusion dates back to the
symbolist period, Gide's treatment in this play of the risk and
irrationalism of Candaule's acts refers, like the 'influence' theme,
to the Nietzschean period immediately preceding the *Nourritures*.
In the words of Candaule:

> . . . posséder, pour moi, c'est expérimenter
> ....
> Risquer! c'est l'autre forme du bonheur.[31]

Gide recalls in his memoirs that earlier period of fervor and
sensual elevation when, in 1895, shortly after the death of his
mother, he experienced a strange, irrational mental state which
would seem strikingly similar to Candaule's attitude towards risk
and experimentation as a means of self-glorification.

> Je vécus les premiers temps de mon deuil dans une sorte d'ivresse morale
> qui m'invitait aux actes les plus inconsidérés. . . . Par exaltation, par
> amour, et *par étrange soif de dénuement . . . j'aurais donné ma fortune
> entière* . . . La seule idée d'une réserve m'aurait paru honteuse et *je
> n'accordais plus audience qu'à ce qui me permit de m'admirer*.[32]

Where Gide, in *Saül*, has depicted the self-indulgence of a
passive " disposition à l'accueil," he has analysed the other extreme
in *Le Roi Candaule*—that of a " donnante nature " guided more
by intellect than emotion and seeking from without both a reflection
of self-fulfillment and a relief from the demands of the moral crisis.
The irrationalism and confusion of Candaule's personality and
the artificial, insincere nature of his acts result from his belief
that knowledge based on illusion and symbol can compensate for
the disorder of the basic self. The psychological conflict, Gide has
discovered, is but further aggravated by the sensual passivity of a
Saül or by the illusory ideas of a Candaule. For the truth lies
beneath the idea and the symbol and it is only through effort and
discipline, personal and unsolicited, that man can promote an inner

---

[30] *T. C.*, II, 76.
[31] *Ibid.*, pp. 77-78.
[32] *S. G. N. M.*, *O. C.*, X, 443-444. Italics added.

harmony and, consequently, a sincerity and gratuity in the external act. The solution lies alone in these terms of Philoctète: " Rien obtenir du dehors . . . mais beaucoup obtenir de moi-même." [33]

2. *Le Retour*

In October 1899, Gide completed for the composer Raymond Bonheur the first act of a light-opera scenario in verse for which Bonheur was to write the musical score. Gide, however, did not carry the play beyond the initial stage. The completed first act contains in its four scenes the nucleus of a typically Gidian plot and character development but is, in itself, perhaps less of a key to an understanding of the author than are the esthetic and moral reasons behind Gide's interruption of the work. This " divergence d'esthétique " between Gide and Bonheur, as described in Gide's correspondence with Bonheur and in his " in memoriam " to the composer,[34] gives us an insight into Gide's conception of the rôle of the dramatist and esthetician and elaborates that theory of artistic dependence on moral harmony which we have already observed in discussing the earlier plays.

Having abandoned his first choice of Balzac's *Duchesse de Langeais,* Bonheur submitted to Gide a new plan for a scenario, *Le Retour,* the first act of which was completed and sent to Bonheur shortly after. ". . . Je suis dans le ravissement "; writes Bonheur on receipt of the manuscript, " c'est parfait . . . infiniment au delà de tout ce que je pouvais espérer et j'en sens clairement maintenant la musique. . . ." [35] Yet this happy collaboration was to be short-lived. It is true that Gide was heavily burdened with his own projects at this time: the preparation of articles and lectures; the publication of *Philoctète* in the *Revue Blanche;* the reorganization of *L'Ermitage* and its demands on Gide for contributions and advice (in January, 1900, he was assigned the bibliographical notes), and that all this—coupled with what he has termed " une exigence toujours plus méchante vis-à-vis de moi-même " [36]— prevented him from devoting his full time to *Le Retour.* However, there were even deeper causes contributing to Gide's break with Bonheur that stemmed from the total incompatibility of the

[33] *T. C.,* I, 159.
[34] Cf. *Le Retour* (1st ed.), Ides et Calendes, 1946.
[35] *Ibid.,* p. 12.   [36] *Ibid.,* p. 56.

esthetic concepts of the two men and which led to Gide's reluctant abandonment of the project in August 1901.

Gide's lecture on "Les Limites de l'art" (1901) sums up his artistic credo at this period:

Dieu propose: c'est le naturalisme, l'objectivisme . . .
L'homme dispose: c'est l'à-priorisme, l'idéalisme.
Dieu propose et l'homme dispose: c'est l'oeuvre d'art.

. . . .

Les *limites* ne sont qu'en l'artiste; heureux celui qui les élargit en lui, les recule et qui, comme devrait vouloir chacun d'eux, *soumet le plus possible à lui, le plus possible de nature.*[37]

The work of art, then, depends on discipline, industry and a balanced, harmonious ethic on the artist's part. It is not involuntary but rational, and neither totally idealistic nor objective in its inspiration. "La beauté ne sera jamais une production naturelle "; Gide writes in "Evolution du théâtre" (1904), "elle ne s'obtient que par une artificielle contrainte." [38]

Bonheur, however, like his friend Francis Jammes, had little patience with the disciplined work of art, laboriously conceived. "La moindre trace d'effort et de contention faisait Bonheur se rétracter "; says Gide, "il n'admettait que spontanéité, qu'abandon . . ." [39] Bonheur does not hesitate to express this divergence of views in a letter to Gide shortly after receiving the latter's lecture on "Les Limites de l'art ":

Je ne peux pas croire que l'oeuvre d'art soit oeuvre volontaire, qu'elle soit oeuvre de raison; je crois qu'un chef d'oeuvre toujours est logique et harmonieux. . . . C'est Dieu seul qui à la fois propose et dispose . . . lui seul est le grand dispensateur de la grâce . . .[40]

Gide makes it quite clear in one of his last letters to Bonheur (Nov. 25, 1925) that the non-completion of *Le Retour* and the resulting compromise of their relationship resulted from the irreconcilable nature of their esthetic views.

La seule raison de mon retrait et de mon silence a été la protection de mon travail. . . . Vous me prêchiez (. . .) une spontanéité un peu trop exempte d'effort, un abandon où je ne pouvais me satisfaire.[41]

---

[37] *O. C.*, III, 408-409.
[38] *O. C.*, IV, 206.
[41] *Ibid.*, p. 107.
In the *Journal* (1905), p. 192, Gide states: " Raymond Bonheur que

[39] *Le Retour* (1st. ed.), p. 14.
[40] *Ibid.*, p. 13.

The scene of *Le Retour* is set in the drawing-room of a bourgeois family in the provinces. Marthe, her younger sister Lucile and their grandfather are anxiously awaiting the return of Marthe's husband, Horace, who has been away on a business venture in North Africa. From the very beginning we are aware that Gide has prepared the stage for a psychological conflict of characters with the patient, confident Marthe and the conservative old grandfather offset by the restless, emotional Lucile and the voyager, Horace.

Lucile, intrigued by the legend of the adventuring Horace, does not share her sister's confidence in his return, her " confiance simple et jamais alarmée." To lend a nostalgic note to the homecoming, Marthe has donned the same dress she wore the day of her husband's departure. Lucile, however, would replace this conventional garb by " une robe plus tendre," one which would dispel the past and provide the voyager with an illusion of renewal and rejuvenation.

> Je changerais de tout, de front et de cheveux.
> Lisant l'oubli d'hier dans mon coeur et mes yeux,
> Il croirait retrouver une femme nouvelle
> Et dirait, plein d'amour plus jeune et plus joyeux:
> Ah! je ne savais plus qu'elle était aussi belle! [42]

Horace arrives and, like Gide after his return from Africa, finds his perspective broadened and his critical judgement enlarged by his travels. " Je ne croyais pas le salon si petit . . ." [43] he remarks quite spontaneously and then vows, on Marthe's insistence, that his wanderings are through and that he will take up again the routine of family life. Yet one senses his impatience with the " foyer clos "; for he knows that the memories of domestic bliss can never rival the more recent joys of a free, unfettered existence. To Marthe's fear that he may have become ill during his stay in Africa, Horace replies in terms which echo Gide's own feelings as recorded in the memoirs and *Journal*:

j'ai revu hier ne comprend pas qu'on se *force*. C'est au contraire mon mot d'ordre. Je souhaite toutes mes branches arquées, comme celles que le jardinier habile tourmente afin de les pousser à fruits."

[42] *T. C.*, II, p. 13.

[43] *Ibid.*, p. 17.

4

> La fièvre à Assouan!? Mais tu n'y songes pas!
> Il n'est pas de terre plus saine.
> On y guérit de tout; le ciel est toujours beau;
> . . . .
> J'ai laissé le soleil; je trouve ici la pluie.
> C'est ici que je vais tomber malade.[44]

Lucile appears and, her timidity given way to curiosity, she proceeds to question Horace on his travels and to revive memories which Marthe and the grandfather would have him forget. He has brought her gifts from far-away places and about each he will tell her a story.

How might Gide have completed the play from this point? It is possible that the remembrance of distant lands and exotic climes, perpetuated by the curiosity of Lucile, could lead Horace to return once more to the scenes of his adventures. But is it not more probable that Horace, like Gide, will attempt to discipline himself to social and family responsibility while maintaining nevertheless the rôle of *inquiéteur*, and that in the manner of the " enfant puîné " in Gide's *Enfant prodigue*, it will be Lucile who will find in the example and encouragement of Horace the strength to set out alone to discover the mysteries of life? That Gide has already conceived the emotional proximity of Horace and Lucile in opposition to the conformity and resignation of Marthe and the grandfather is apparent from the closing dialogue of the act:

HORACE:	A chaque objet je vous conterai son histoire . . .
	J'ai rapporté pour vous dans une étroite cage
	Un petit écureuil des îles jaune et noir . . .
MARTHE:	Venez prendre le thé
LUCILE:	Quand pourrai-je le voir?
	Où l'avez-vous laissé? . . .
GRAND-PÈRE:	Allons, venez. Venez! [45]

Gide's unwillingness to complete this scenario according to the time specifications and esthetic notions of Bonheur attests again

[44] *Ibid.*, p. 18.

One recalls here the statement of the narrator in the *Nourritures* referring to Gide's recovery in the African sun: " Je tombai malade: je voyageai. . . . Je renaquis avec un être neuf, sous un ciel neuf et au milieu de choses complètement renouvelées."—*O. C.*, II, 71.

[45] *T. C.*, II, 25-26.

to his individualism and discipline as a creative artist. This unfinished work, written at a time of intense psychological crisis for Gide, shows again that the fruition of the work of art and the "dénûment" of the personality remain inseparable and interdependent. For, as Gide writes many years later: "L'art commence à la résistance: à la résistance vaincue. . . . Aucun chef-d'oeuvre qui ne soit laborieusement obtenu." [46]

3. Bethsabé [47]

The Biblical story of David's passion for Bathsheba, wife of Uriah the Hittite, provides Gide with the theme of his next play, Bethsabé, three scenes in verse, in which we find the disillusionment of Gide's symbolist period—as depicted earlier in the lovers of the Tentative amoureuse—and, as well, the two somewhat conflicting theses of the Nourritures: the first, that sensual elevation lies more in the search for an ideal than in its possession; the second, that God and Pleasure are synonymous and instantaneous. Gide here is once again approaching the problems of his protagonist critically and clinically in terms of his own subjective conflict.

Where in the Biblical account David incurs the wrath of God after his sin against Uriah's wife, Gide's David is deprived of God's grace at the outset of the play. This initial portrait of a confused and lonely king, dispossessed of divine guidance, completes the reader's association of David with Gide himself and accentuates the value of the play as a psychological document. For Gide, too, as we have seen, while still suffering the remorse of conscience, has become estranged from the ways of the Puritan God and is searching for a rational solution to his moral problem. The obstacles which cause David to fall short of his search represent

---

[46] "Préface à une anthologie," Poétique (1948), p. 68.

"L'attente, il en fera une règle," writes Emile Gouiran. "Il attend la révélation qui s'organise au-dedans de lui, par lui. L'équation qui le réalisera, il sait qu'elle se pose dans le silence."—André Gide: Essai de psychologie littéraire, p. 72.

[47] Martin-Chauffier believes Bethsabé was written in 1903 (O. C., IV, x.) but the more likely date is 1902 or even before (T. C., II, 180-181). Scenes I and II appeared in 1903 in the Jan. and Feb. numbers of L'Ermitage and the complete play in Vers et Prose (déc. 1908—mars 1909). The original edition was published in 1909 by the Bibliothèque de l'Occident. The play is dedicated to Mme Lucie Delarue-Mardrus.

the same sensual, destructive urges which Gide is struggling to overcome and which he believes must be continually distinguished from the constructive, rational forces that promote a " dénûment " and fulfillment of the self. The mystic, sensual climate of pro- longed adolescence must be gradually replaced, through immense personal effort, by a more permanent, adult ethic. For, as Gide later observes of this perplexing period of moral transition: " Ce qui permet le lyrisme de l'enfance, c'est l'illusion. *Tout mon effort a été d'obtenir en moi un bonheur qui se passât d'être illusoire.*" [48]

> And it came to pass at eventide, that David arose from his bed, and walked upon the roof of the king's house: and from the roof he saw a woman bathing; and the woman was very beautiful to look upon.[49]

So begins the Biblical account. Gide's play departs from the same point yet the principal character has been transformed and humanized from the God-fearing warrior of the Scriptures and of Gide's *Saül* into a lonely, tortured man who, abandoned by Jehovah, has assumed a position not unlike Gide's earlier characterization of Saül. Both seek relief from loneliness in sensual gratification; both are eager to regain the favor of God, and both fear the censure of the conscience as symbolized by the sorcerers of Saül and, in David's case, by the prophet Nathan. However, where Saül awaits the revelation of Heaven through the stars and must therefore fill a passive and hopeless rôle, Gide introduces, in *Bethsabé*, a con- structive and meaningful solution to man's plight in the form of the symbolic dove—Christian representation of the Holy Ghost.[50] The dove has appeared in David's palace. He has but to seize it to hear once more the word of God and find peace from his sufferings and confusion. As David recounts his adventure to Joab:

> Au-dessus de mon lit l'Esprit de Dieu battait de l'aile,
> Il descendait toujours plus près.

---

[48] *Journal* (1931), p. 1052. Italics added.

[49] II Samuel 11: 2.

[50] Gide's inclusion of Christian iconography in an Old Testament theme is probably explained by the Arabic version of the David-Bathsheba story. This had been revealed to him earlier by his servant, Athman. " Selon la tradition arabe, c'est en poursuivant une colombe d'or de salle en salle . . . que David . . . parvint enfin à cette terrace supérieure d'où il pouvait voir Bethsabé."—" Feuilles de route," *Journal* (1896), p. 80.

Colombe d'or, ma main te saisira peut-être . . .
J'étendis le bras vers l'oiseau;
Puis m'élançai, le poursuivant de salle en salle
. . . .
Il repartait; il bondissait de marche en marche;
Je voulais le saisir et n'osais . . .
Jusqu'où tu monteras, colombe,
J'atteindrai là . . .[51]

Then David stops, unable to muster the strength and discipline to pursue his quarry, and becomes again the victim of illusion and the senses. From the terrace where he had pursued the dove, his eyes fall on Bethsabé, a crouched, white figure reclining in a neighbouring garden.

Oui, cela s'agitait, cela palpitait comme une aile;
Quelques instants, je crus que j'avais retrouvé mon oiseau.[52]

The beauty of Bethsabé has become identified in David's mind with the dove of God as the object of his quest; in his eagerness to forego the trials of the search he has readily confused *Dieu* and *Bonheur*, the permanent and the transitory. He has, indeed, put into practice that recurring theme of the *Nourritures* which Gide now recognizes as false and destructive: " Ne distingue pas Dieu du bonheur et place tout ton bonheur dans l'instant." [53] David's possession of Bethsabé quickly dispels both the illusion of happiness and the fervor of desire and brings with it an awakening to what Hytier terms, " l'inutilité des joies mal acquises." [54]

Elle était mieux dans son jardin
Quand dans la source elle se baignait nue.
Bethsabé! Bethsabé . . . Es-tu la femme? es-tu la source?
Objet vague de mon désir.
Joab, quand dans mes bras enfin je l'ai tenue, .
Le croirais-tu, je doutai presque si ce que je désirais c'était elle . . .[55]

David has sinned, as Gide has sinned, and must face again the censure of an uncompromising God through his servant, Nathan. Yet, if Gide criticizes here the recourse to illusion and the evasion of effort and responsibility, there is present, too, an element of

[51] *T. C.*, II, 155-156.
[52] *Ibid.*, p. 156.
[53] *O. C.*, II, 73.
[54] *André Gide*, p. 25.
[55] *T. C.*, II, 162.

reproach for the vengeful, impersonal Jehovah who demands an unerring virtue of man yet denies him the warmth and consolation of his love. ". . . Que fera l'homme," asks David, " si derrière chacun de ses désirs se cache Dieu ? " [56] Gide will find the answer, as we shall see, not in the Puritan God but in a personal humanized Christ—the Christ of the Prodigal Son who, by rationalizing the paradox of individualism and self-sacrifice, will bring David's " colombe d'or " within reasonable access of man.

Fundamentally, however, the individual must act alone, and patience, discipline and restraint remain his sole means of self-realization and the surest safeguards against the escapism and short-sightedness of a Candaule or a David. Perhaps nowhere is this essential psychological distinction between Idea and Truth, symbol and reality more clearly expressed than in these words of Lessing, quoted by Gide in the *Journal*:

> Ce qui fait la valeur de l'homme, ce n'est pas la vérité qu'il possède, ou qu'il croit posséder; c'est l'effort sincère qu'il a fait pour la conquérir. Car *ce n'est point par la possession, mais par la recherche de la vérité que l'homme grandit ses forces et qu'il se perfectionne.*[57]

4. *Ajax* [58]

Ajax, Gide's reinterpretation of a Sophoclean theme, was begun in 1904 but abandoned some three years later in an unfinished state comprising only a single short scene of prose dialogue between Ulysses and Minerva.

At the outset of the Sophocles play, the arms of Achilles—which had been claimed by Ajax as the most valorous of the Greek warriors—have instead been awarded by the Atridae to Odysseus on the pretext that such a prize in the hands of the arrogant and ambitious Ajax would endanger the unity of the Greek armies. When Ajax, in a mad fit of rage, leaves his tent to avenge himself on the Greek chieftains, Athena, his patron goddess whom his pride has estranged, deludes him into mistaking for his enemies the sheep and cattle of the camp. As the play opens, Athena is discussing the plight of Ajax with her favorite, Odysseus. She warns

---

[56] *Ibid.*, p. 165.

[57] *Journal*, p. 52. Italics added.

[58] First published in 1933 by Gallimard in vol. IV of the *Oeuvres complètes.*

him against any similar display of arrogance and independence and demands his complete loyalty and subservience to the will of the gods.

Gide's play also begins with a dialogue between Ulysse (Odysseus) and Minerve (Athena) but with this difference: the recipient of Achilles' arms has not yet been determined and it is Ulysse who must make the final decision. On this account he has sought the advice of Minerve, but the goddess—and this is an original Gidian interpretation—seems determined (quite unlike the Athena of Sophocles) to withhold her opinion and to promote, rather, a free and independent judgement on his part:

Le sage qui demande conseil n'attend pourtant point du dehors l'inspiration de sa conduite; mais, exposant les motifs de son incertitude, il trouve la leçon qu'il quêtait, à les développer clairement.[59]

While Gide has found in the relationship of Ulysse and Minerve an opportunity to stress the ideal of independent judgment, we know, from his characterizations in *Philoctète*, that he is quite out of sympathy with the unerring devotion-to-state attitude of Ulysse. This viewpoint of Ulysse is revealed in the following exchange wherein Minerve ironically suggests the injustice of the situation:

M: C'est donc une autorisation des dieux que tu souhaites: la permission de passer outre et *de considérer l'intérêt avant la justice.*

U: *Oui; l'intérêt de tous, avant le contentement d'un seul.*[60]

Ulysse still hesitates to formulate his desire to thwart Ajax' possession of the arms and continues to rationalize his position in the hope that Minerve will assume full responsibility for the final decision. However, the goddess deliberately upholds a contrary opinion to goad Ulysse into committing himself. " Mais l'arc d'Achille ne doit-il pas revenir au plus fort? " she argues. " J'admire, Ulysse, que tu viennes quêter des dieux, et ne saches t'accorder toi-même cette autorisation, si tu crois la mériter." [61] Finally, however, this subtle questioning by Minerve leads Ulysse to a completely independent, self-made assertion.

[59] *T. C.*, II, 172.
[60] *Ibid.*, p. 173. Italics added.
[61] *Ibid.*, p. 174.

M: Le conseil que tu réclamais, tu te le donnes toi-même.

U: Peut-être, causant avec toi.[62]

One can only surmise as to the reasons for Gide's inability to carry this play beyond the first scene. In a *Journal* entry for 1904, he confesses he has been unable to work seriously since completion of *L'Immoraliste* (Oct. 25, 1901). " Un morne engourdissement d'esprit me fait végéter depuis trois ans. . . . La moindre phrase me coûte. . . ." [63] This confused state of mind would account partly for the non-completion of *Ajax* whose characters had so little affinity with actual or potential urges of Gide's nature and could therefore represent, only very incompletely, an externalization of the inner dialogue. This theme offered Gide neither the catharsis of self-identification and evaluation, such as he had found in the treatments of *Saül* and *Candaule,* nor the consoling ideal and constructive ethic he had discovered in *Philoctète.*

Having exhausted the theme of independent judgement in his interpretation of the Ulysse-Minerve dialogue, Gide was no doubt faced with the dilemma of delineating the character of Ajax in the following scenes. The madness of the Greek warrior following the award of the arms would have to be developed in any version of the legend and would be the logical outcome of Ulysse's decision in the early development of Gide's play. Yet how was the author to reconcile the holocaust wrought by an insane, irrational Ajax with that ideal of spiritual independence already associated in the opening scene with a sane and rational Ulysse? That Gide may well have envisaged the problem in these terms finds support in a *Journal* entry for 1907:

> J'ai voulu me remettre à *Ajax,* mais, examinant mieux le sujet, je crains ne pouvoir expliquer, excuser même le geste d'Ajax sans intervention de Minerve ou de la folie; il faudrait les deux à la fois: pratiquement absurde (il l'est suffisamment) et, idéalement, admirable (il ne l'est point). —Rien à faire.[64]

One possible solution would have been to subordinate Ajax and continue Ulysse as the central figure of the drama. This, however, would have been both esthetically and morally impossible for Gide at this point in his evolution. First, it would likely have opened

---

[62] *Ibid.,* p. 176.   [63] *Journal,* p. 144.   [64] *Ibid.,* p. 241.

his play to political implications (and to any such objective treatment he was clearly opposed!) by suggesting an opposition between the will of the state and the rights of the individual, issues which—arising out of the Dreyfus Affair—had aroused universal concern at the turn of the century. Secondly, and most important, it would have been morally impossible for Gide to extend his admiration of Ulysse's act of independence in the first scene to include an acceptance of the motivations underlying his attitude to Ajax: that of an authoritarian philosophy to which Gide as individualist and humanist was diametrically opposed. Were Gide to have accepted the thesis of individual subjugation to the gods, he would, in fact, have been contradicting his own increasingly intense aversion to Puritanism and weakening his growing faith—soon to be manifested in the *Enfant prodique*—in the humanistic qualities of Christ.

During this period of deep moral searching, Gide is more than ever convinced of those two essential psychological truths, as inherent in the humanism of a Montaigne or a Goethe as in the teachings of the Gospels: the one, that the individual must find within himself the key to his own salvation; the other, as stated by Gide: " Que chacun soit plus précieux que tous." [65] Gide's Ulysse had, with difficulty, affirmed the first principle but had strongly denied the second. Nor would Ajax have been a fitting spokesman for such theses. For the enemy, with divine approval, had already laid the plans for his defeat and he was, at the close of Gide's first scene, much as Odysseus pictures him at the outset of the Sophocles play: " bound, hand and foot, to fatal destiny." [66]

---

[65] " Préface à *Armance*," *O. C.*, XI, 81, note 2.
[66] *Sophocles* (tr. by F. Storr), II, 19.

CHAPTER IV

EVASION AND RENUNCIATION

1. The Rôle of Christ in the Moral Conflict

It has perhaps been shown in the last chapter how the moral conflict with which Gide was faced in the years following the completion of *L'Immoraliste* was largely responsible for his non-completion of the plays, *Le Retour* and *Ajax*. He now faces a similar difficulty with his *récit, La Porte étroite*, which leads him to interrupt its composition in 1907. Yet it is highly significant that in just two weeks, in February 1907, he was able to compose, to his complete satisfaction, *Le Retour de l'enfant prodigue*—one of his most profound and revealing works where, he admits, " pour la première fois l'exécution a suivi immédiatement la conception." [1]

Gide was no doubt dissatisfied with the negative, critical philosophy which, with the exception of *Philoctète*, had dominated his writings since *Saül*, and wished to offer a constructive solution to the moral problem, to strike an optimistic balance between the unrestrained hedonism of a Michel and the excessive abnegation of an Alissa. This need was answered in his dialogues on the parable of the Prodigal Son which not only represent a fundamental change in his moral philosophy and a crystallization of his religious views but constitute, as well, one of the most gratuitous and subjective works of his career. In the words of Paul Claudel, *L'Enfant prodigue* is " l'ouvrage . . . qui me donne le plus de jour sur votre âme et sur votre pensée." [2]

That this play corresponds to a more intense search on Gide's part for moral harmony is apparent from the correspondence and *Journal* entries of this period. " Je pars demain," he writes to Raymond Bonheur in 1903 on the eve of a trip to Africa. " Cet équilibre heureux que vous dites avoir trouvé et que je vous envie

---

[1] *Journal* (1907), p. 240.

[2] *Correspondance, Claudel-Gide*, p. 83.

.`. . je n'ai pu le trouver ici." [3] And again, in the *Journal* for 1905, we read:

Rien ne se tient, rien n'est constant dans ma vie . . . me sentant porté soudain de l'un à l'autre extrême, dans ce balancement même, je sens que ma fatalité s'accomplit.[4]

The dualism of his nature had become intensified by the earlier introduction of satanic, sensual urges to combat the " part de Dieu." Yet his hope, voiced on his departure for Algeria in 1893, that this " dualisme discordant " might eventually be resolved and integrated,[5] had become less and less of a reality. The implacable doctrine of the Puritan God could lead only to a refusal of life and a denial of the being; the dominance of Satan, on the other hand, would sacrifice the personality to hedonism and sensual illusion. The coexistence of conscience and emotion, of the Puritanical and the satanic could be of constructive value, both morally and esthetically, only if the two basic, psychic contrasts were reconciled through a rationalization of their main elements : constraint and individualism. Gide feels very deeply, then, the growing need for a full accord in the dialogue, for relief from the remorse and suffering of the Puritan conscience in constant debate with the immoralism of a Ménalque. As Gide writes many years later of this crisis :

. . . c'est par personnelle expérience que je savais combien on s'use, et combien en vain, dans la lutte, une lutte que j'avais entretenue entre les éléments les plus opposés de ma nature, jusqu'au jour où je me suis dit : à quoi bon ? où j'ai cherché non plus la lutte et le partiel triomphe, mais l'accord. . . .[6]

This reconciling force Gide finds not in the Zeus of Philoctète or the Jehovah of Saül but in the person and teachings of the New Testament Christ—the Christ of the parables, symbol of both emancipation and renunciation and, to Gide, the only ideal whereby the anarchy of the inner dialogue could be resolved and a progress towards the " dénûment " attained.

As Gide had found encouragement in Nietzsche for his revolt from Puritanism and an example of serviceable individualism in Goethe, it is in Dostoyevsky that he finds his greatest inspiration

---

[3] *Le Retour* (1st. ed.), p. 83.
[4] *Journal*, p. 174.
[5] Cf. *S. G. N. M.*, *O. C.*, X, 348.
[6] " Feuillets," *Journal*, p. 1294.

during this period of Christian reorientation. Gide is an avid reader of Dostoyevsky at this time and is to complete, immediately after the *Enfant prodigue*, his essays on " Dostoïevsky d'après sa correspondance " (1908). He is perhaps most impressed and consoled by Dostoyevsky's personal, emotional concept of Christ, by " ce bonheur, cette joie par delà la douleur, qu'on sent latente dans toute la vie et l'oeuvre de Dostoïevsky." [7] Dostoyevsky's psychological struggle Gide sees as a parallel to his own; in Dostoyevsky's belief that the contradictions between individualism and abnegation are reconcilable, he finds hope for the solution of his own crisis. And he envisages the solution to Dostoyevsky's problem, and to his own, in the light of that famous Christian maxim which he will so often evoke in the years to come: " Cette solution, le Christ le lui enseigne: ' *Qui veut sauver sa vie la perdra; qui donnera sa vie pour l'amour de moi la rendra vraiment vivante.*' " [8]

In addition to satisfying the spiritual and moral needs of its author, *Le Retour de l'enfant prodigue* stands as Gide's reply to his critics, and particularly to Claudel and Jammes who, sceptical of his wavering on the religious issue, were anxious to win him over to the Catholic fold. Claudel's letters to Gide prior to 1907, the date of *L'Enfant prodigue*, reflect the former's intransigent support of Catholicism and his eagerness to dissuade Gide from his pagan learnings and convert him to the ways of the church.[9] In a work written in 1906, *Abrégé de toute la doctrine chrétienne* (a copy of which was immediately forwarded to Gide!) Claudel writes in terms which are soon to be emphatically contradicted by Gide: ". . . la Vérité catholique s'apprend le mieux . . . par le placement de toute notre personne dans son ordre vrai . . ." And again, in a letter to Gide, dated March 14, 1906, just before his departure for China, Claudel speaks of " la vérité qui réside uniquement dans les enseignements de l'Eglise catholique, et non pas ailleurs. Admettez dans votre coeur cette irruption du fait," he exhorts Gide, " faites place dans votre intelligence à d'immenses espaces déserts." [10] Gide, however, refuses to submit to these arguments and is determined to evolve his own position independent of

---

[7] " Dostoïevsky d'après sa correspondance," *O. C.*, V, 69-70.

[8] *Ibid.*, p. 69. Italics added.

[9] Cf. *Correspondance, Claudel-Gide*, p. 45 ff.

[10] *Ibid.*, p. 66.

external influence or established systems. That this persuasive technique of Claudel was an important factor in Gide's formulation of a new ethic is sustained by a revealing letter to Christian Beck, written a few months after the completion of *L'Enfant prodigue*:

Peut-être ne savez-vous pas que Claudel, après avoir trouvé en Jammes une brebis facile à ramener au Seigneur, a voulu m'entreprendre à mon tour. . . . Il ne se dissimulait sans doute pas qu'avec mon hérédité et mon éducation protestante il n'avait pas tâche facile; n'importe, il s'obstina, encouragé jusqu'à l'excès par la très vive sympathie que je montrais pour son oeuvre. . . .[11] Jammes . . . me fit entendre qu'un article de lui . . . allait célébrer ma conversion. . . .

Tout de même, comprenant jusqu'au fond des moelles *l'intérêt* du geste que Claudel et lui souhaitaient me voir faire, et pourquoi je ne le faisais pas—et comment, si je l'avais fait, ce n'eût pu être qu'à la manière dont *mon* Enfant prodigue rentra à la *maison*, et pour aider à en sortir le petit frère—j'écrivis cette petite oeuvre ' de circonstance ' où j'ai mis tout mon coeur, mais aussi toute ma raison.[12]

That Gide's period of negative, self-critical works should have led him to the Old Testament and his search for a more optimistic, constructive ethic to the New Testament seems reasonable enough from a moral and psychological standpoint. Yet there is, as well, an esthetic attraction to the Gospels and the teachings of Christ to which he is acutely sensitive and which cannot be disregarded in considering his inclusion of a new moral philosophy within the framework of a Christian parable. As he writes to one of his critics in later years:

Je puis trouver dans les paraboles du Christ plus de poésie que dans Homère; il ne m'en paraîtrait pas moins irrévérencieux de parler du Christ comme d'un artiste, ou de présenter certaines de ses paraboles dans un livre de ' morceaux choisis.' [13]

The answer to a moral and spiritual crisis, the reply to criticism and influence and the satisfaction of an esthetic sense: *Le Retour de l'enfant prodigue* is all these. Here, for the first time, Gide succeeds in striking a balance between the contrasting ethics of

[11] In February and April 1907, Gide corrected the proofs of Claudel's *Art poétique* and his *Connaissance de l'est* during the poet's absence at the French consulate in Tientsin.

[12] " Lettres à Christian Beck," *Mercure de France*, CCCVI, (août 1949), p. 621. Gide's letter is dated July 2, 1907.

[13] " Lettre au R. P. Victor Poucel," *O. C.*, XIV, 409.

Michel and Alissa, of paganism and Puritanism, and in blending together his own moral extremes into a constructive work of art.[14] Above all, this work stands out as a revelation of Gide himself, as a gratuitous externalization of his inner emotions and contrasts— one where, by his own admission: "... je tâche à mettre en dialogue les réticences et les élans de mon esprit." [15]

2. *Le Retour de l'enfant prodigue* [16]

Gide's Prodigal Son returns home disillusioned by the search for a Christian " dénûment ": "... il n'a pas trouvé le bonheur, ni même su prolonger longtemps cette ivresse qu'à défaut de bonheur il cherchait." [17] Unable to bear the discomforts of the trip after his heritage has been squandered, he turns back to the security of the past and the pleasures of the fatted calf. Here, as with the David of *Bethsabé*, we find again the pantheistic association of *Dieu*, *Plaisir* and *Bonheur* that was developed earlier in the *Nourritures*. Yet this theme is carried an important step forward here through the Prodigal's admission that only in suffering and hardship did he feel the presence and nearness of his father who, as the symbol of Christ, is here identified not with possession but with penury and abnegation.

PRODIGUE: Dans ce dénûment, je me suis senti près de vous, Père.

PÈRE: Fallait-il la misère pour te pousser à revenir à moi?

PRODIGUE: Je ne sais, je ne sais. C'est dans l'aridité du désert que j'ai le mieux aimé ma soif.[18]

---

[14] " L'esthetique d'André Gide (dont *Le Retour de l'enfant prodigue* offre un exemple typique) apparaît comme l'harmonisation de deux tendances, de deux visions logiquement inconciliables, de ce qu'il appelait lui-même l'élément chrétien et l'élément païen."—Ramon Fernandez, *André Gide et notre temps*, p. 14.

[15] *Journal* (1907), p. 237.

[16] These five *tableaux* in prose were written in the latter part of February, 1907, and appeared first in *Vers et Prose* (mars, avril, mai, 1907). The same review published the original edition in 1907. The dialogues were first presented in dramatic form, as a play, by Ides et Calendes in vol. III of the *Théâtre complet*. The dedication is to Arthur Fontaine, French sociologist and economist.

[17] *T. C.*, III, 14.

[18] *Ibid.*, p. 20.

Nor can God be found in pleasure alone or even in the search for pleasure, but lies always ahead, like the Prodigal's father, in the form of a compassionate and forgiving Christ.

PÈRE: Pauvre enfant! Je t'ai parlé peut-être durement. Ton frère l'a voulu: *ici c'est lui qui fait la loi.* C'est lui qui m'a sommé de te dire: 'Hors la maison, point de salut pour toi.' Mais écoute: c'est moi qui t'ai formé; ce qui est en toi, je le sais. Je sais ce qui te poussait sur les routes; *je t'attendais au bout. Tu m'aurais appelé . . . j'étais là.*

PRODIGUE: Mon Père! j'aurais donc pu vous retrouver sans revenir? . . .[19]

The anticlerical meaning is quite apparent in this treatment of the forgiving father, the stern, moralistic brother and the impatient, searching Prodigal. The " hors la Maison, point de salut " principle of the Frère Aîné represents the dogmatism and restraint of organized religion which, according to Gide, misinterprets the teachings of Christ and prevents the moral and intellectual growth of the individual. ". . . Moi je suis dans l'ordre; tout ce qui s'en distingue est fruit ou semence d'orgueil," [20] says the Frère Aîné in terms which provide an ironically accurate preview of that very orthodox Catholic reaction of Paul Claudel when, on receipt of the *Enfant prodigue*, in March 1908, he writes: " qui n'est pas contenu dans l'édifice de Dieu, il est enfermé dans les limites affreusement étroites de l'amour propre. . . ." [21]

The tragedy of Gide's Prodigal lies in his inability to advance toward a Christian self-denial and in his return to the lethargic, closed system of the older brother wherein the words of Le Père, of Christ the emancipator, are falsified and misconstrued to meet the needs of the " Maison."

AÎNÉ: Je sais ce que te dit le Père. C'est vague. Il ne s'explique pas très clairement; de sorte qu'on lui fait dire ce qu'on veut. Mais moi je connais bien sa pensée. Auprès de ses serviteurs j'en reste l'unique inter-prète et qui veut comprendre le Père doit m'écouter.

PRODIGUE: Je l'entendais très aisément sans toi.[22]

Gide is now convinced that salvation lies not within the house

---

[19] *Ibid.*, p. 22. Italics added.
[20] *Ibid.*, p. 24.
[21] *Correspondance, Claudel-Gide*, p. 84.
[22] *T. C.*, III, 25.

and church, as his critics Claudel and Jammes believe, but rather in a revolt from these restrictive institutions and a renewal of life in the ideal of Christian renunciation.[23] Christ, then, must neither be confined to a system or dogma nor confused with sensual elevation. He lies as the goal and not as the beginning of man's struggle. He stands, like the Prodigal's father, " au bout," as encouragement for both evasion and abnegation. For only by a prior emancipation from the absolute values of the *status quo* can man be born again in single loyalty to the Christian ideal and set forth, with hope of success, through what Gide has called " the last gateway " to life and adventure.[24]

When, as early as 1897, Gide had written of this need for separating Christ from the confines of organized religion, he was voicing a personal feeling which the demands of the emotional crisis were later to elaborate more completely in *L'Enfant prodigue.*

On en viendra bientôt, je pense, à dégager les paroles du Christ, pour les laisser paraître plus émancipatrices qu'elles ne le paraissaient jusqu'alors. Moins ensevelies, elles paraîtront plus dramatiques, niant enfin la famille (. . .) tirant l'homme lui-même de son milieu pour une carrière personnelle et lui enseignant par son exemple et par sa voix à n'avoir plus de possessions sur la terre. . . .[25]

Had the Prodigue realized that Christ, Le Père, lay ahead of him and not behind, in the loneliness of the desert and not in the security of the home, he would have found courage to continue the search and would not have suffered, as had the Gide of *Paludes,* from the realization of his " dissemblance." Gide's concept of the Prodigal's father is, indeed, the first clear indication of what is to become his definitive religious philosophy: that of the " Dieu à venir "—a view he develops fully in *Dieu, fils de l'homme* (1942) but which is first formulated at the height of his religious crisis in 1916.

Si j'avais à formuler un credo, je dirais: Dieu n'est pas en arrière de nous. Il est à venir. C'est non pas au début, c'est à la fin de l'évolution des êtres qu'il le faut chercher. Il est terminal et non initial. C'est le point suprême et dernier à quoi tend toute la nature dans le temps.[26]

---

[23] Seigneur! celui qui vient à Vous n'a plus de maison." — *Numquid et tu . . . ?, Journal,* p. 597.
[24] *Les Nourritures terrestres, O. C.,* II, 161.
[25] " Réflexions . . .," *O. C.,* II, 431.
[26] *Journal,* p. 533.

The Enfant Prodigue has failed, but his young brother will succeed, profiting from the example and shortcomings of the Prodigal. Nor will the " ivresse " of possession weaken his fervor and desire for the " dénûment." He will depart completely free of all material and family attachments, already reconciled to the trials of the journey. And at the end of the play, he sets out alone, like so many of Gide's heroes, to make his way in life and to discover the essence of his being.

The dialogue of the parting brothers reminds one again of Gide's parting admonition to his disciple Nathanaël of the *Nourritures terrestres* (a consistent attitude with Gide but one frequently overlooked by the critics of his so-called ' immoral ' influence on youth) : " Nathanaël, jette mon livre. . . . Ne crois que *ta* vérité puisse être trouvée par quelque autre : plus que de tout aie honte de cela." [27] Such, too, is the reaction of Gide's Prodigal Son to his young brother's departure :

PUÎNÉ : Tu m'as ouvert la route, et de penser à toi me soutiendra.

PRODIGUE : A moi de t'admirer : à toi de m'oublier, au contraire . . .

. . . .

PUÎNÉ : Mon frère . . . Pars avec moi.

PRODIGUE : . . . Sans moi tu seras plus vaillant . . . Sois fort; oublie-nous; oublie-moi. Puisses-tu ne pas revenir . . . Descends doucement. Je tiens la lampe . . .[28]

Gide has now discovered the key to a moral philosophy independent of both Puritanism and Catholicism, one which closes the gulf between Prometheus and Zeus and between David and Jehovah by bringing God closer to man through the teachings of a personal, humanized Christ.

" Le catholicisme est inadmissible. Le protestantisme est intolérable," he writes in 1912. " Et je me sens profondément chrétien." [29]

The explanation of this new and emphatic assertion lies in the *Enfant prodigue.* For there Gide has found, at last, a rational formula for the reconciliation of his psychic contrasts. Where *Saül,*

---

[27] *O. C.,* II, 223. Referring again in later years to his rôle as *influenceur,* Gide writes : " L'influence que j'ai pu souhaiter est toute émancipatrice : c'est d'encourager chacun dans son sens, et de différer de moi le plus possible."—" Feuillets," *O. C.,* XIII, 444.

[28] *T. C.,* III, 46-47.

[29] *Journal,* p. 367.

5

Candaule and *Bethsabé* had given a negative and critical appraisal of the moral problem, the *Enfant prodigue*, without rejecting the evasion theme of the *Nourritures*, represents Gide's first practical and constructive advance towards that ideal of self-fulfillment announced earlier in *Philoctète*. In this play, Gide has supplemented and fused the earlier Nietzschean ethic of individualism and revolt with the Christian principle of renunciation. To the self-centered, hedonistic evasion of the *Nourritures* he has added the message of the New Testament with a view to discovering: "dans l'oubli de soi la réalisation de soi la plus parfaite, la plus haute exigence, et la plus illimitée permission de bonheur." [30]

---

[30] "Préface de l'édition de 1927," *Les Nourritures terrestres, O.C.*, II, 229.

Chapter V

HUMANISM AND THE GIDIAN SYNTHESIS

1. Moral Integration and Objectivity

If Gide's *anxiety* in the years preceding the *Enfant prodigue* was essentially psychological and subjective, it would seem that his moral crisis during the years 1914-18 (he did not publish a single work during this period) was of a more impersonal and objective nature. In the *Enfant prodigue* the moral question still predominated. There was no suggestion of social concern or participation on the part of the protagonists. During the war years, however, Gide could not but consider the plight of those about him and the disturbing gulf which lay between the ideals of Christian charity and goodwill and the cruel realities of the day.

An accumulation of many social experiences was to contribute to the growingly objective and humanistic current which pervades Gide's work in the post-war years. In 1896, he had served as mayor of a commune in Normandy; in 1912, as a juror in Rouen (*Souvenirs de la Cour d'Assises*). In 1914-16, he worked among the sick and needy at the Foyer franco-belge, and in 1925-26 was absent on a special mission for the Colonial Ministry, later incorporating his observations in the *Voyage au Congo* and the *Retour du Tchad*. Both these works condemned social injustices in the African colonies and led to restrictive measures against the exploitation of the native population by industrial monopolies.

Where Gide's works from *Saül* to the *Enfant prodigue* illustrate a deeply personal concern for the moral and religious problem, the writings after 1920 show, then, an increasing interest in the social question, a closer observation of reality and a greater association of characters and ideas with the contemporary scene. This new approach is particularily apparent in *Les Faux-Monnayeurs* (1926) wherein Gide provides for the first time an objective synthesis of modern life rather than the analysis of a single psychological extreme. This is true, too, as we shall see, of his plays of this new era: *Oedipe, Perséphone, Le Treizième Arbre* and *Robert ou l'Intérêt général.*

This substitution of the humanistic and the social for the mystic and metaphysical might well be interpreted as a sign that Gide has succeeded, to a considerable extent, in rationalizing his own crisis. He has, through a harmonization of his psychic contrasts, achieved a sufficient " dénûment " of the personality to allow an evolution from introversion and self-analysis to a more objective study of man. A more terse and lucid style seems evident, too, in the works after 1920—a fact which can perhaps be attributed, in part, to the loss of that intensity and complexity which had produced the richer, more poetic form of such plays as *Saül* and *Philoctète.* The various tendencies of the inner dialogue have been externalized, one by one, in his theatre: the narcissism of Saül, the gratuitousness of Philoctète, the irrationalism of Candaule, the illusionism of David and the restlessness of the Enfant Prodigue. Writing to André Rouveyre in 1924, Gide speaks of the moral catharsis worked through the diversity and subjective analysis of his writings. Referring to his earlier anxiety and unrest he states:

Je le serais sans doute encore, si je n'avais pas su *délivrer mes diverses possibilités dans mes livres et projeter hors de moi les personnages contradictoires qui m'habitaient.* Le résultat de cette purgation morale, c'est un grand calme; osons le dire: une certaine sérénité.[1]

With this greater integration of the moral conflict there comes, as well, the turning of the artist from the mirror of the self to the spectacle of his surroundings. "Je me suis complètement désintéressé de mon âme et de mon salut," he remarks to Claudel. " De même dans la vie, c'est la pensée, l'émotion d'autrui qui m'habite. . . ." [2] And it is not long before Claudel himself, whose self-styled rôle as confessor and converter of the *literati* had been enhanced by Gide's earlier spiritual crisis, is forced to admit failure before this non-Catholic solution of the Gidian conflict and the resulting concern for human and social values on a non-mystic and nonmetaphysical plane. In reference to what was to be their last interview (May 1925) Claudel reluctantly observes:

[1] *Lettres*, p. 32. Italics added.
[2] *Journal des Faux-Monnayeurs, O. C.*, XIII, 49.

Il me dit que son inquiétude religieuse est finie, qu'il jouit d'une sorte de *félicité*, basée sur le travail et la sympathie. Le côté *goethien* de son caractère l'a emporté sur le côté chrétien.[8]

Through effort, experience and, most important of all, through the analysis and evaluation in the work of art of each of his fundamental psychological tendencies, Gide is now largely reconciled to his moral perplexities and is ready to consider social, religious and political themes on the basis of actuality and in terms of humanistic and practical values. " Acceptation ; confiance ; sérénité : vertus de vieillard," he writes in 1927, and adds as if to paraphrase the experience of his counterpart, Bernard Profitendieu: " L'âge de la lutte avec l'ange est passé." [4]

This new social consciousness clearly evidenced in Gide's plays of this period coincides, therefore, with a critical attitude towards capitalism, an outspoken anticlericalism and an enthusiasm for the communist experiments in Russia. Where, at the time of *Saül*, Gide had insisted on the pre-eminence of the moral over the social,[5] he takes the reverse position in 1931 when the play *Oedipe* was first performed :

J'ai longtemps professé que la question morale devait prendre le pas sur la question sociale; il ne me paraît plus à présent. . . . L'individu, encore aujourd'hui, m'intéresse plus que la masse; mais d'abord importent les favorables conditions de la masse pour permettre à l'individu sain de se produire.[6]

2. *Oedipe* [7]

The plays of the 1930's provide a *mise au point* of this new orientation of Gide's thought. The farce, *Le Treizième Arbre,* pokes fun at the clergy and aristocracy ; *Robert ou l'Intérêt général,* socialist and anticlerical in theme, deals realistically with labor-capital relations and the poetic *Perséphone* offers a symbolic fusion of the " part de Dieu " and the " part de Satan " through the

[8] *Correspondance, Claudel-Gide*, p. 242.

[4] *Journal*, p. 842.

[5] " Reflexions . . ." *O. C.*, II, 423.

[6] *Journal*, p. 1135.

[7] Three acts in prose written between January 1 and November 9, 1930, *Oedipe* was first published in 1931 by Editions de la Pléiade. The dedication is to Bernard Groethuysen, philosopher-critic and a fervent communist.

sympathy of a goddess for an oppressed Underworld. It is in *Oedipe,* however, that we find what is perhaps the clearest synthesis of Gide's views on moral development and social progress, closely associated with his own experience but linked through dialogue and characterizations to present-day life. Observation of contemporary morals and satire of French society and social institutions; a strong anticlericalism and critique of the concept of an all-responsible, transcendental divinity and, finally, the humanistic solution to the enigma of man: these are the three basic themes of the play, each of which should be examined in turn.

Gide makes it clear in the *Journal* that his aim is not to rival the pathos and " grand style " of Sophocles' *Oedipus tyrannus* but rather to evoke in his reader a curiosity and an intellectual response to his interpretation of the myth in a modern light.

Il y a dans les plaisanteries, trivialités et incongruités du mien, comme un besoin constant d'avertir le public: vous avez la pièce de Sophocle et je ne me pose pas en rival; je lui laisse le pathétique . . . c'est à votre intelligence que je m'adresse. Je me propose, non de vous faire frémir ou pleurer, mais de vous faire réfléchir.[8]

Where the pre-Socratic morality of Sophocles necessitated the total submission of the individual to the gods, Gide represents his hero as a rationalist and humanist and as spokesman for his now familiar thesis of independence and self-assertion. As Philoctète and Ulysse had found the truth through their own initiative, so too does Gide's Oedipe through his flouting of the divinity (he prefers the provocative questions of the Sphinx to the cold responses and judgments of the oracle) and through his independent discovery and expiation of his own crime. Oedipe's personal discovery of his guilt is developed with greater force and concentration by the omission of those lesser characters of the *Oedipus tyrannus*: the two messengers and the herdsman of Laïus whose function in the Greek play was to provide Oedipe with a network of facts from

---

[8] *Journal* (1933), p. 1151.

A production of *Oedipe* by the director Hartung at Darmstadt in June 1932 cleverly stressed the many anachronisms of the play and thereby clarified Gide's intellectualization and modernization of the myth. Modern costumes were used and a paradoxical effect obtained by the décor: the juxtaposition of the columns of a Greek temple with a projection on a rear curtain of Notre-Dame de Paris.

which he might readily deduce his true position. The basic difference between the Sophocles and Gide versions, however, lies in the fact that whereas in the Greek play curiosity and self-assurance led to the downfall of Oedipus, those same elements in Gide's hero promote his liberation from the past and the fulfillment of his personality in a final act of integrated and constructive individualism.

Complementing the independent and sceptical Oedipe in Gide's play are the principal characters of the legend cast in a modern mold: Tirésias, the stern, Puritanical pastor; Jocaste, the moral hypocrite; Antigone, symbol of intellectual sincerity; Créon, the traditionalist and political opportunist; and Etéocle and Polynice, symbolizing the confusion and amoralism of post-war youth. The chorus, too, renounces its traditional decorum and splits in two to air the views of the conservative and liberal sides of public opinion. Freudian undertones in the dialogue of the children and frequent modernisms, parodies and puns [9] both heighten the humorous, ironic relief and complete the illusion of the contemporary scene.

Gide's views on the gullibility and conformity of the masses are well summed up in the constant censure given the individualist Oedipe by the assembled chorus:

Nous, Choeur, qui avons pour mission particulière, en ce lieu, de représenter l'opinion du plus grand nombre, nous nous déclarons surpris et peinés par la profession d'une individualité si farouche. Les sentiments qu'exprime Oedipe ne se supportent chez autri que déguisés.[10]

The attitude of the chorus in its whimpering subservience to the gods and to the traditional moral and political systems, its distaste for the rational and the unique is largely determined, Gide feels,

[9] " tu nous a fichus dedans " (*T. C.*, IV, 70), " je m'en fous " (p. 89), " si je te foutais mon poing sur la gueule " (p. 89) ; " il y a quelque chose de pourri dans le royaume " (p. 67) ; " on peut dire qu'il s'est mis là dans de mauvais draps " (p. 106), etc.

A revealing note on Gide's stylistic principles in this period of increased objectivity and social concern is found in a letter to Paul Souday, 13 oct. 1923, *O. C.*, XI, 118-119; " Il importe que la langue écrite ne s'éloigne pas trop de la langue parlée . . . J'estime qu'il est vain, qu'il est dangereux, de se cramponner à des tournures et à des significations tombées en désuétude, et que céder un peu permet de résister beaucoup."

[10] *T. C.*, IV, 65.

by the omnipotent rôle assumed by the church as arbiter of public morals. The progress of the individual as well as of society and government is indeed difficult when, as Oedipe puts it: "Le peuple préfère toujours à l'explication naturelle l'interprétation mystique." [11]

The apathy and conservatism of Créon represents "cette force d'inertie et de cramponnement" which, as evidenced in the reactionary elements of French post-war politics was, Gide believed, a dangerous obstacle to social reform and initiative. And Créon, of course, rationalizes his attitude—as would the leader of any present-day rightist group—as a necessary counterbalance to the more liberal, progressive views of an Oedipe or a Gide. With this characterization of Créon, Gide transposes on a political plane that same independence of the Catholic-traditionalist philosophy that he had earlier formulated from a religious viewpoint in his *Enfant prodigue*. How readily Gide might have had a Massis or a Béraud in mind when he makes Créon remark to Oedipe:

A toi, l'initiative, la nouveauté. Quant à moi, le passé me lie. Je respecte la tradition, les coutumes, les lois établies. Mais ne penses-tu pas qu'il est bon, dans un Etat, que tout cela soit représenté, et que je fais, en regard de ton esprit novateur, un heureux contrepoids qui te retienne d'aller trop vite, qui mette un frein à tes entreprises trop hardies, lesquelles risqueraient souvent de disloquer le corps social, si l'on ne leur opposait cette force d'inertie et de cramponnement qui est mienne? [12]

In Etéocle and Polynice we find the cynicism, self-pity and would-be *libertinage* which beset a considerable segment of French youth in the years following the First World War—as, indeed, it had developed a century earlier in the Romantic *mal du siècle* of the post-Napoleonic era. Etéocle, who has written a book entitled *Mal du Siècle*, with the subtitle, *Notre Inquiétude*,[13] maintains that literature is most effective when it can provide "l'approbation de l'indécence" and remarks cynically that readers are constantly searching for "des apophtegmes, des théories, qui mettent leur conscience à l'aise et de leur côté le bon droit." [14] Yet, when he

---

[11] *Ibid.*, p. 70.　　　　　　　[12] *Ibid.*, p. 80.

[13] This is a parody of a book and an article written by two of Gide's disciples: *Notre Inquiétude* by Daniel-Rops and "Un Nouveau Mal du siècle" by Marcel Arland.

[14] *T. C.*, IV, 88.

states within his father's hearing that he himself is seeking an authorization for incest with his sister, Ismène, Oedipe remarks in terms which, despite their tragic irony in the context of the play, represent a fundamental Gidian ethic:

Mes petits, respectez vos soeurs. Ce qui nous touche de trop près n'est jamais bien profitable. Pour se grandir, il faut porter loin de soi ses regards.[15]

If the term ' cosmic irony ' can be defined as the expression of an individual's revolt against the supernatural coupled with an indictment of the tedium and inertia of human life,[16] then it is clearly this form which dominates and sharpens the anticlerical thesis of Gide's *Oedipe*. This attitude, as an outgrowth of modern rationalism, was not, of course, a characteristic of the Greek theatre with its predominantly authoritarian, non-relativist psychology. And here, again, we have a further divergence between the philosophic and social treatment of Gide and the ' terror and pity ' formula of his Sophoclean model. The essential theme of his play, Gide insists, is less in the opposition of free-will and predestination than in the struggle between individualism and the submission to religious authority. The conflicting philosophies of Oedipe and Tirésias (whom Gide has transformed from his original rôle of kindly sage into a dogmatic, short-sighted bigot) serve to emphasize the gulf between naturalism and mysticism, individuality and group-thinking and to satirize both the stagnation of a traditionalist society and the absolutism of organized religion. A clear indication of Gide's growing antipathy to the clergy and of his more humanistic, practical approach is found in the *Journal* for 1927 when he was first considering a new treatment of the Oedipus legend.

Le palais de la foi. . . . Vous y trouverez consolation, assurance et confort. Tout y est ménagé pour protéger votre paresse et garantir l'esprit contre l'effort.

' Nourri dans ce palais, j'en connais les détours.' . . . Il faut laisser trop de choses au vestiaire. J'abandonne volontiers ma bourse, mais non pas ma raison—ma raison de vivre.[17]

Oedipe's ignorance of his parentage, like the revolt from family

---

[15] *Ibid.*, p. 91.
[16] Cf. David Worcester, *The Art of satire*, pp. 127-137.
[17] *Journal*, p. 837.

and tradition of the Enfant Prodigue and of Bernard of the *Faux-Monnayeurs*, is, to Gide, a decided advantage in the human, individualistic solution of the moral problem. This attitude of complete independence before God and family contrasts sharply with Gide's earlier concern for the Puritan conscience as reflected in Saül's fear of the sorcerers and David's submission before the prophet Nathan.

> Jailli de l'inconnu [says Oedipe]; plus de passé, plus de modèle, rien sur quoi m'appuyer; tout à créer, patrie, ancêtres . . . à inventer, à découvrir. Personne à qui ressembler que moi-même . . . O Créon! si soumis, si conforme à tout, comment comprendras-tu la beauté de cette exigence? C'est un appel à la vaillance . . .[18]

Since for Gide morality is an individual and not a universal problem, the solution to the enigma of the Sphinx must come from within through effort and discipline and a humanistic rejection of the gods and fates. Oedipe's advice to his sons sums up Gide's own problem and illustrates, as well, his new social consciousness and faith in human progress:

> J'imagine, beaucoup plus tard, la terre couverte d'une humanité désasservie, qui considérera notre civilisation d'aujourd'hui du même oeil que nous considérons l'état des hommes au début de leur lent progrès. Si j'ai vaincu le Sphinx, ce n'est pas pour que vous reposiez . . . J'ai compris, moi seul ai compris, que le seul mot de passe, pour n'être pas dévoré par le Sphinx, c'est l'Homme. . . .
>
> Car, comprenez-moi bien, mes petits, que chacun de nous, adolescent, rencontre, au début de sa course, un monstre qui dresse devant lui telle énigme qui nous puisse empêcher d'avancer. . . . persuadez-vous . . . qu'*il n'y a qu'une seule et même réponse à de si diverses questions; et que cette réponse unique, c'est: l'Homme; et que cet homme unique, pour un chacun de nous, c'est: Soi.*[19]

Oedipe has conquered the material Sphinx. However, he does not actually advance to the " dénûment " until he has solved the enigma within himself: until he has realized that he himself is the murderer of Laïus and that his life with Jocaste has been based on error and ignorance. " Dans la crainte de Dieu gît mon pouvoir. Son bonheur tranquille est impie," Tirésias says of Oedipe.[20] Yet this tranquillity and self-satisfaction of Oedipe—encouraged by the monotonous, effortless court life and by the deceit and hypocrisy

---

[18] *T. C.*, IV, 82.   [19] *Ibid.*, p. 92. Italics added.   [20] *Ibid.*, p. 74.

of Jocaste and the courtiers—quickly disappear the moment that
reason and logic lead him to doubt his own infallibility. Near the
end of the play as the truth finally dawns on him, he remarks:
" Oedipe, le temps de la quiétude est passé. Réveille-toi de ton
bonheur." [21] Like the awakening of Gide's critical judgement with
Saül and his rejection of the irrational ethic of the *Nourritures*,
so, too, Oedipe evolves from a "bonheur tranquille" to a more
honest and realistic appraisal of his own position. ". . . Je ne
pouvais plus dépasser qu'en prenant élan contre moi-même," [22]
Oedipe admits in terms which recall the destruction by Prométhée
of that obstacle to self-realization: the 'vulture-conscience.' [23] But
where Prométhée's had been an act of liberation and revolt (in
keeping with the then Nietzschean ethic of Gide), Oedipe's is,
as well, an act implying self-sacrifice and abnegation. His blindness
—self-inflicted and gratuitous—achieves what the *Journal* calls:
" cette abnégation qui accompagne toute noblesse." [24] But while
this element of Christian abnegation predominates, there is present,
also, that complementary urge of pagan gratuity—one which has a
striking parallel in the self-destruction of Dostoyevsky's Kirillov,
who would thereby affirm his independence of Providence. As Gide
quotes Kirillov in his *Conférences sur Dostoïevsky* (1922), it would
almost seem as if he were already aware of the analogy between the
suicide of Dostoyevsky's hero and the self-blinding of his own
Oedipe.

' Si Dieu existe, tout dépend de lui, et je ne puis rien en dehors de sa
volonté. S'il n'existe pas, tout dépend de moi et je suis tenu d'affirmer
mon indépendance de la façon la plus complète. Je suis tenu de me brûler
la cervelle.' [25]

Similarly, Oedipe refuses to ascribe to the gôds the responsibility
for his crime lest he compromise his faith in his own will and free
choice as an individual. And he remarks before committing his
' acte gratuit ':

[21] *Ibid.*, p. 97.

[22] *Ibid.*, p. 109.

[23] " Il me mangeait depuis longtemps; j'ai trouvé que c'était mon tour."—
Le Prométhée mal enchaîné, O. C., III, 158.

[24] *Journal*, p. 1006.

[25] *O. C.*, XI, 300.

Ah! je voudrais échapper au dieu qui m'enveloppe, à moi-même. Je ne sais quoi d'héroïque et de surhumain me tourmente. Je voudrais inventer je ne sais quelle nouvelle douleur. Inventer quelque geste fou, qui vous étonne tous, qui m'étonne moi-même, et les dieux.[26]

Oedipe's self-blinding is an individualistic urge, not an act of remorse or of sacrifice to the divinity, for a god who would wish man to commit a crime unknowingly and unintentionally is unworthy of sacrifice. It represents, as well, an abnegation of the self which, as in the case of Philoctète, results in an exaltation of the whole being and a greater integration of the personality.

Unlike the pathetic and remorseful Oedipus of Sophocles who is driven into exile, the departure of Gide's hero is entirely voluntary and self-willed.[27] The illusory happiness of Candaule and David is past as is the smug individualism of Ménalque and Michel. Oedipe, " qui renonce à ses biens, à sa gloire, à soi-même," sets out (not unlike Sartre's *engagé* hero of *Les Mouches*) to carry his message to mankind. " Que t'importent ceux qui ne te connaissent pas ? " asks the chorus. And Oedipe replies: " Quels qu'ils soient, ce sont des hommes. Au prix de ma souffrance, il m'est doux de leur apporter du bonheur." [28]

With the self-sacrifice and voluntary exile of Oedipe, Gide affirms his faith in the dignity and independence of man; in assigning to his hero a social mission, he affirms his belief that it is not Providence but only man—free and unfettered by dogma, tradition and superstition—who holds the key to human betterment and social progress. As Gide writes in his *Feuillets d'automne* of 1947:

Mais l'homme ne peut-il pas apprendre à exiger de soi, par vertu, ce qu'il croit exigé par Dieu ? Il faudra bien pourtant qu'il y parvienne; que quelques-uns, du moins d'abord; faute de quoi la partie serait perdue. Elle ne sera gagnée, cette étrange partie que voici que nous jouons sur terre

---

[26] *T. C.*, IV, 105.

[27] The oracle's prophecy that prosperity awaited those among whom Oedipus died is revealed in the *Oedipus Coloneus* after the hero's arrival at the court of Theseus at Athens. Gide, however, introduces this fact *before* Oedipus' departure from Thebes. His voluntary exile, despite the entreaties of the people of Thebes that he remain, thus constitutes a further act of independence and individualism.

[28] *T. C.*, IV, 111.

... que si c'est à la vertu que l'idée de Dieu, en se retirant, cède la place; que si c'est la vertu de l'homme, sa dignité, qui remplace et supplante Dieu.[29]

3. Perséphone [30]

In 1933, at the request of Ida Rubinstein, Gide wrote the three tableaux of an opera scenario in verse entitled *Perséphone*. In 1904, he had developed a blue-print of the same theme: *Proserpine*, which he envisioned then as a dramatic symphony in four tableaux. The later, completed version (where the Latin forms Proserpine and Ceres are replaced by the Greek Persephone and Demeter) is more profound and meaningful and, at the same time, more concise than the original outline.[31]

As late as 1922, Gide had stated his distaste for the *mélange* of artistic genres, for the synthesis of the arts as prescribed by Wagner.[32] That he should have written *Perséphone* as a vehicle for the fusion of music, dance and dialogue and, too, as a further representation of his new humanistic philosophy, is further proof of this broader, less restricted esthetic which we have already associated with a more mature and stable psychology.

In this symbolic union of Heaven and Hell, Gide achieves on an artistic plane that reconciliation of contrasts and antagonisms which has for so long been the goal of his own moral struggle. In this synthesis of opposites we find, as well, a pluralistic, universal perspective of life which supplants the unique, particular analyses of the earlier works and presents, as Gide says of his *Faux-Monnayeurs*: " un carrefour—un rendez-vous de problèmes." [33]

Homer's *Hymn to Demeter* recounts how Persephone (Kore) is carried off to the Underworld by Hades (Pluto), how the earth's harvests suffer as Demeter, goddess of the fruits of the earth, wanders

---

[29] *Feuillets d'automne*, pp. 271-272.

[30] First published by Gallimard in 1934, *Perséphone* is dedicated to Ida Rubinstein " dont la ferveur a su ranimer un projet endormi depuis plus de vingt ans."

[31] *Proserpine* (first published in *O. C.*, IV, in 1933) had speaking rôles for Cérès, Pluton, Calypso, Eurydice and the choruses. The dialogue of *Perséphone* is assigned only to Perséphone, to Eumolpe (legendary founder of the mysteries of Eleusis who serves here as narrator) and to the choruses of Nymphes, Enfants, Danaïdes and Ombres.

[32] Cf. *Journal des Faux-Monnayeurs*, *O. C.*, XIII, 40.

[33] *Journal*, p. 760.

about in search of her daughter, and how Zeus finally persuades Pluto to release Persephone who, having tasted the seed of a pomegranate, is obliged to spend some time of every year among the shadows of the lower regions. Gide's plot follows the essentials of this Homeric hymn but develops the human and social possibilities of the legend by transforming his heroine, Perséphone, into something of a social crusader whose visits to and departures from the Underworld represent more a genuine concern for the sufferings of humanity than a mechanical, duty-bound response to a ' contract ' with Pluto or to the dictates of Olympus. Where the Persephone of legend is carried off forcibly by Pluto, Gide's goddess leaves voluntarily, filled with pity for: " Tout un peuple sans espérance / Triste, inquiet, décoloré." [34] For as she played with the nymphs, she had seen in the flower of the narcissus a vision of the misfortunes of Hell. (Homer had referred to the narcissus as revealing not Hell but Heaven—" tout l'Ouranos étoilé," as Gide translates it.[35]) Perséphone's concern for the creatures of the Underworld long precedes, then, in Gide's version, her tasting of the pomergranate and establishes, at the outset of the play, that social, humanitarian thesis Gide wishes to stress. As Perséphone replies to the nymphs who beg her to remain with them on earth:

> Comment pourrais-je avec vous, désormais,
> Rire et chanter, insouciante,
> A présent que j'ai vu, à présent que je sais
> Qu'un peuple insatisfait souffre et vit dans l'attente.
> O peuple douloureux des ombres, tu m'attires,
> Vers toi, j'irai . . .[36]

After a short stay in Hades, it is a vision of earth, cold, devastated and anxious for the return of Spring which appears to Perséphone in the flower of the narcissus. Nor does the pomegranate —food of the Dead—which Gide had earlier represented as the fruit of desire in the *Nourritures* (" Ronde de la grenade ") and as a symbol of the exotic in the *Enfant prodigue*, obscure her contemplation of earth's famine and distress. And so she leaves to join Déméter and her earthly husband, Triptolème, and to resume for a time her rôle as queen " du terrestre printemps et non plus des Enfers." [37]

---

[34] *T. C.*, IV, 121.   [36] *T. C.*, IV, 122.
[35] *Proserpine, T. C.*, IV, 144.   [37] *Ibid.*, p. 132.

With the return of Perséphone and Spring, the earth prospers
and brings forth a full harvest. But with the approach of winter,
the goddess feels again the need to depart for the Underworld,
motivated, as before, only by pity and goodwill for the oppressed.

> Crois-tu qu'impunément se penche sur le gouffre
> De l'enfer douloureux un coeur ivre d'amour?
> J'ai vu ce qui se cache et se dérobe au jour
> Et ne puis t'oublier, vérité désolante.
> Mercure que voici me prendra consentante.
> *Je n'ai pas besoin d'ordre et me rends de plein gré*
> *Où non point tant la loi que mon amour me mène*
> *Et je veux pas à pas et degré par degré,*
> *Descendre jusqu'au fond de la détresse humaine.*[88]

In 1923, Gide had translated *The Marriage of Heaven and Hell*
of William Blake. Fifteen years later he writes in the *Journal* of
his own " constant besoin de conciliation," and adds: " Je voudrais
marier le Ciel et l'Enfer, à la Blake; réduire les antagonismes." [39]
Surely that very union and synthesis to which he refers has been
reached in this little play where Earth and Hades are, in a sense,
blended with Heaven through their mutual dependence on the love
and sympathy of the goddess Perséphone. This work is an application, too, of that esthetic principle of universality and totality
in the work of art which Gide has summed up in his lectures on
Dostoyevsky (and appropriately so there, for the broad, humanistic
pattern of his later works owes much to Dostoyevsky's influence):
" Oui, vraiment, toute oeuvre d'art est un lieu de contact . . . un
anneau de mariage du ciel et de l'enfer." [40]

---

[88] *Ibid.*, p. 137. Italics added.
[39] " Feuillets," *Journal*, p. 1293.
[40] *Conférences sur Dostoïevsky, O. C.*, XI, 280.

CHAPTER VI

SATIRE AND THE SOCIAL CONSCIENCE

1. From Subjective Irony to Social Satire

In one of his " feuillets,"- written about 1923, Gide refers to all his writings—with the single exception of the *Nourritures terrestres*—as " ironiques " and critical, as comprising separate analyses of single psychological extremes.[1] The relationship between Gide's mental struggle and the conflicting tendencies of a Michel or an Alissa has already been discussed. However, the deep-set irony in Gide's works prior to 1925 has a close connection not only with the subjectivity of his characterizations but also with the introspection, the searching and the subtle innuendo—developing from his own psychological crisis—which dominate his writings during that period. The *Nourritures* is, admittedly, subjective but, written as it was at a time of moral exaltation and self-satisfaction, it is too confident, too fervent [2] and too little critical to encompass the restraint and the ' time-lag ' one normally associates with an ironical composition. If neither irony nor, for that matter, satire can be ascribed to the *Nourritures*, its fervor and enthusiasm and its absence of moral and psychological searching find an echo in Gide's approach to his last two plays: *Le Treizième Arbre* and *Robert ou l'Intérêt général*. For where enthusiasm for life and the joys of the senses inspired the *Nourritures*, an enthusiasm of a less subjective and more social kind—but one equally devoid of moral self-searching—underlies his writing of these two plays. And here it is satire, objective and direct, (with a substantial flavoring of farce and burlesque in the case of *Le Treizième Arbre*) which replaces the more complex, subjective and indirect method of the earlier, ironic works.

[1] Cf. " Feuillets," *O. C.*, XIII, 439-440.
[2] " L'ironie est le contraire de la ferveur," writes Hytier, *André Gide*, p. 91.

More deliberate and outspoken in their satire of clergy and aristocracy than was the case with *Oedipe*, these plays, through the very directness and objectivity of their satire, show again the extent to which Gide has succeeded in overcoming and rationalizing his own moral disturbances. However, they reflect, above all, the socialistic, pro-communist viewpoint held so strongly by Gide in the years 1930-1936.[3]

" Tout mon coeur applaudit à cette gigantesque et pourtant toute humaine entreprise," he writes in 1931 of Russian communism [4] (although still admitting that esthetically he remains part of an intellectual elite unable to share the artistic tastes of the general public). As Gide will later realize, after his trip to Russia in 1936, his leftist feelings represented more a " communisme de l'esprit," as Archambault puts it, than a " communisme de la lettre." [5] Prior to this, however, he somehow believes Russian communism to be compatible with individualism and that through its theoretical equality of rights and its aversion to both capitalist monopolies and organized religion it best exemplifies the principles of emancipation and service inherent in his own concept of Christ's teachings.[6]

The church and the moneyed classes come in for the brunt of the attack in these plays and the satiric content (despite the burlesque and frankly comic aspects of *Le Treizième Arbre*) contradicts Gide's restatement, in 1932, of an earlier esthetic: that social and utilitarian considerations should be foreign to the work of art. His statement at that time: that he would prefer to write nothing at all " plutôt que de plier mon art à des fins utilitaires," [7] is by no means borne out by these two plays which, indeed, illustrate clearly his intense interest in social and economic issues throughout the early 1930's.

---

[3] " Lu, depuis quelques mois, quantité de livres, presque tous ayant trait aux questions économiques et sociales, à la crise actuelle."—*Journal* (juillet 1932), p. 1136.

Gide's orientation during this whole period is summed up in the title *Littérature engagée* given to a collection of his extra-literary writings from 1930-1938. (Gallimard, 1950).

[4] *Ibid.*, p. 1047.   [5] *Humanité d'André Gide*, p. 243.

[6] *Journal* (1933), p. 1176: ". . . ce qui m'amène au communisme, ce n'est pas Marx, c'est l'Evangile."

[7] *Ibid.*, p. 1149.

As Jean Hytier has observed, there is both a negative and positive
side to every satire and the true meaning of the satiric work can
be fathomed only by distinguishing "à travers les objets de sa
raillerie . . . les affirmations de la morale. . . ." [8] This is particularly
true of Le Treizième Arbre and L'Intérêt général, for behind their
satire one can perceive a seriousness of purpose and a basic consciousness of human and social values. As Gide writes in 1935
when the composition of these plays was already underway:

> Je me laisse persuader aujourd'hui que l'homme même ne peut changer
> que d'abord les conditions sociales ne l'y invitent et ne l'y aident—de
> sorte que ce soit d'elles qu'il faille d'abord s'occuper. [9]

2. Le Treizième Arbre

Le Treizième Arbre, a plaisanterie in one act, was written in the
early months of 1935 and intended as a " lever de rideau " for
Georges Pitoëff who had been the producer, in 1931, of Gide's
Oedipe. [10] Within these five short scenes of social farce built about
a theme of Freudian psychoanalysis, Gide directs a deft little
satire against clergy and aristocracy and the alliance of both groups
in opposition to the ' moderns ' and non-conformists.

An austere country chateau has as its normal inhabitants the
Comtesse, the Vicomte (her son) and an English governess, Miss
Plot, charged with the correct upbringing of the Vicomte's offspring.
Their peaceful, rural routine, whose moral well-being is solicitously
guarded by Le Curé, becomes suddenly endangered by the arrival
of three very urbane and sophisticated guests: Armand, nephew of
the Comtesse, and his friends: Le Philologue (M. Lavignette) and
Le Docteur-Psychanalyste (M. Styx).

As the plays opens, the Vicomte is about to leave the chateau
but with some misgivings, for the Curé has warned him of the
unorthodox views held by Armand and his group and of their
" propos irrévérencieux contre la croyance et les vérités." [11] To
the despair of the Curé, the somewhat credulous Comtesse has
already become intrigued by her guests. Imaginative and escapist

---

[8] Op. cit., p. 94.

[9] Journal, p. 1241.

[10] Le Treizième Arbre was never presented by the Compagnie Pitoëff.
It was first produced in May 1935 by the Rideau Gris of Marseilles.

[11] T. C., V, 140.

by nature, she dislikes reading or discussing social themes and contemporary problems and much prefers to ignore " les misères que nous ne pouvons pas secourir." [12] For that reason, the revelations of M. Lavignette concerning the weirder aspects of Greek mythology and the suggestive symbols and drawings of ancient cave dwellers provide most exciting fare for the imagination and a minimum strain on the intellect. Yet she is more reticent about M. Styx (psychiatrists love to uncover *problems!*) and the possibility that through psychoanalysis he might unearth " un tas de vilaines choses que j'aime mieux ignorer." [13] However, the determined Freudian, M. Styx, is genuinely fond of disturbing the uninitiated and proceeds with a familiar Gidian view: that excessive repression of the passions and the subconscious is harmful; that the *refoulement* of contemporary man is to be deplored and that the more balanced psychology of the ancient Greeks resulted from their more ready acquiescence to the dictates of passion. The ensuing dialogue establishes the Comtesse as a most provocative subject for the psychiatrist's couch:

PHILOLOGUE: Les Oedipes de nos jours ne sont peut-être pas moins nombreux qu'autrefois. L'inceste par exemple est très fréquent dans les campagnes.

COMTESSE: Je vous assure, Docteur, que . . .
. . . .

DOCTEUR: Mais, la plupart du temps, de nos jours, Oedipe n'épouse plus sa mère. Il se contente de la convoiter.

COMTESSE: Docteur, vous abusez de ce que mon fils est absent . . .[14]

The Curé, meanwhile, has become greatly upset by the situation, less through concern for the 'corruption' of his faithful charge than through fear that these brash intruders might replace him in her affection and endanger his future participation in the good life of the château—not to mention his frequent visitations of the wine cellar. Despite all his efforts, the guests continue their

[12] *Ibid.*, p. 143.

[13] *Ibid.*, p. 144.

It is unlikely that Gide was acquainted with Freud's work before 1922. " Freud. Le freudisme . . . Depuis dix ans, quinze ans, j'en fais sans le savoir."—*Journal* (4 février 1922), p. 729.

[14] *T. C.*, V, 147-148.

'demoralization' of the Comtesse. The latter is particularly impressed by the Philologue's description of primitive religions and the "culte des arbres" ("J'ai toujours adoré les arbres," she states in a delightfully ironic confession [15]). And why should she feel shocked by M. Lavignette's nice collection of pre-historic engravings? After all, ". . . les femmes vraiment honnêtes n'ont pas à se montrer pudibondes." [16] Surely Freud would have found here an interesting test-case to support his theories on the correspondences between the psychology of primitive races, as taught by folklore, and the psychology of the neurotic as revealed through psychoanalysis. In referring to the controlling principle of primitive nature philosophy or animism as "omnipotence of thought," Freud adds:

> Only in one field has the omnipotence of thought been retained in our own civilization, namely in art. In art alone it still happens that man, consumed by his wishes, produces something similar to the gratification of these wishes, and this playing, thanks to artistic illusion, calls forth effects as if it were something real.[17]

The discovery of an obscene drawing carved on a tree bordering the main driveway of the estate (tree no. 13, according to the gardener Boccage) provides the Curé with hopes of retaliation against his rivals. Such a diabolical creation—a gnome-like creature in a vividly unconventional pose—must certainly, the Curé believes, have been perpetrated by the newcomers. To make the crisis even more degrading, the innocent children had been observed in the area and even the prim Miss Plot had been found seated serenely at the foot of the tree, "en contemplation." "Oh! c'est du beau travail," says the gardener Boccage. "C'est même on peut dire . . . fignolé." [18] This enthusiasm for the artistic merits of the work is not, however, shared by the Curé who, profiting from the moral shock of the Comtesse and fortified by a few glasses of liqueur, assumes immediate control of the situation. Concluding that the tree had been "déshonoré" between four and six the previous afternoon, he eagerly launches an inquiry into the where-

---

[15] *Ibid.*, p. 150.
[16] *Ibid.*, p. 151.
[17] *Totem and Taboo: Basic Writings*, p. 877.
[18] *T. C.*, V, 157.

abouts of the guests at that time. Notwithstanding a summons from the sick-bed of a parishioner, the old cleric refuses to leave the scene until his inquisition has unmasked the culprit. When no one can recall his exact whereabouts at four o'clock—the time of the crime—the Comtesse cheerfully responds to Armand's suggestion that she read aloud from the diary where she has, as usual, noted the detailed happenings of the previous day. The Comtesse proceeds to outline the activities of each member of the group and refers to her own decision, at precisely four o'clock, to take a stroll in the château grounds. At this point, her voice falters and she faints away. And so the case is solved to the hilarity of Armand and company but to the painful embarrassment of the Curé.

The final scene centres on the Curé's efforts to reassure the Comtesse of her purity and innocence. The philologist and psychoanalyst are entirely to blame, insists the Curé as he downs a glass of brandy. Milady is by no means a " femme perdue " but simply a defenseless victim of suggestion and immoral conversation.

The Vicomte returns to find Armand's friends busily applying coats of white paint to the depraved tree-trunk and summarily dismisses them as vagrants and pranksters. The entire incident is, of course, attributed to these wicked gentlemen and Armand, the ringleader, is roundly upbraided for his mockery of convention and precedent: " Je t'aime bien, tu le sais," the Vicomte tells him, " mais depuis que tu fréquentes ces bolcheviks, je t'entends professer des opinions que je tiens pour déplorables." And the old Curé, firmly entrenched once more, crowns his triumph and ends the play with a final word of old-guard censure to the ' delinquent ' youth:

Que ceci vous serve de leçon, mon cher Armand. Toutes ces belles théories modernes, vous le voyez, ne résistent pas à l'épreuve. Vous nous reviendrez amendé.[19]

The meaning of this play is obvious enough and there is little room for interpretation or analogy. However, what it reveals of Gide's talent as a dramatist of the farcical and the burlesque in society and of his appreciation of the humorous possibilities of psychoanalysis should not lead one to overlook the anticlerical and antiaristocratic bias underlying the basic theme of the play. The

[19] *Ibid.*, p. 168.

year 1935—when this play was written—was a particularly active one for Gide; it was a time when social and political activities almost completely overshadowed his literary concerns. Support of Russian life and culture, denunciation of Fascism and Facist persecution of communist leaders: these are among the main themes revealed in his correspondence, articles and lectures for that year. As joint-chairman (with André Malraux) of an international congress of pro-communist writers, in June 1935, Gide maintained in a lecture, " Défense de la Culture," that the survival and advancement of the arts depended, above all, on social and economic progress. A society which repressed liberalism and held blindly to the conservative traditions of the past was a threat to culture, he argued. For, " les ennemis de la culture sont ceux qui se font les apologistes du mensonge, et . . . de l'état social mensonger dans lequel nous vivons." [20] It is this same conservatism—fostered by the aristocracy and the church—which Gide ridicules in *Le Treizième Arbre*, in the old-fashioned ways of the Comtesse and her retinue, in their reluctance to accept new ideas and in the casuistry and hypocrisy of the parish priest.

Despite its gaiety and charm, there is not in this play the strictly humorous intent that one might attribute to the comedies of a Feydeau or a Courteline. *Le Treizième Arbre* is, certainly, a *plaisanterie* but it is, too, as Raymond Lepoutre has remarked: " une plaisanterie où le refoulement freudien . . . sert de prétexte à une attaque habile contre la religion." [21]

3. Robert ou l'Intérêt général [22]

The writing of *Robert ou l'Intérêt général* extends over the period 1934-1940 when, as we have seen, Gide was intensely preoccupied with social issues and when an idealistic and sentimental enthusiasm for the communist state was supplanted, in turn, by a

[20] *Littérature engagée*, p. 90.

[21] *André Gide*, p. 86.

[22] Five acts, in prose, the play first appeared in the review *l'Arche* in 1944-45 (nos. 5, 6, 7, 8). *Ides et Calendes* published the first edition in 1949 as vol. VI of the *Théâtre complet*.

The fact that this play has as a main theme the close relationship of a hypocritical industrialist and a Catholic priest suggests a possible anti-clerical key to the *Intérêt général* of the title. One of Gide's most out-

vigorous and realistic renunciation of the original pro-Russian attitude.

The first version of the play—completed between 1934 and 1936 —corresponded to what Gide has termed " ma ' lune de miel ' avec le parti communiste " and represented views " d'une allure nettement tendancieuse." [23] The play in this first form of pro-communist *littérature engagée* was translated into Russian and would have been presented on the Moscow stage but for a sudden reversal of opinion on Gide's part. A visit to Russia, in the summer of 1936, brought him a rude awakening to the evils of the Marxist state and the realization that an irreparable gulf lay between his own communistic idealism—clinging to a faith in human dignity and social justice—and a political system fostering regimentation and the suppression of free thought. He returned to France as bitterly opposed to the dogma and orthodoxy of Soviet communism as he was to the social abuses of capitalism. " Du train dont va l'U. R. S. S.," he writes in 1937, " tout ce que nous blâmons le plus dans le régime capitaliste va bientôt se trouver restauré." [24]

Believing that the extreme views of his earlier development of *L'Intérêt général* no longer represented his new more practical and reasoned approach to the social problem, Gide worked painstakingly between 1938 and 1940 on a complete revision of the work with a view to subordinating the social thesis through greater concentration on character portrayal. The play as we know it today is, then, the result of those two years of revising and correcting the original document.

An immediate analogy that comes to mind on reading *Robert ou l'Intérêt général* is the resemblance between the couple Robert and Eveline of Gide's *L'Ecole des femmes* (1929) and the Robert and Laure of this play. Both husbands are hypocritical, pompous

---

spoken Catholic critics was Victor Poucel, a priest. (Cf. *Etudes*: nos. dated 5 and 20 Oct., 1927, and *L'Esprit d'André Gide*: Lib. de l'Art catholique, 1929). In a letter to Poucel, in 1927, Gide writes: ". . . rien ne m'a plus averti contre le catholicisme que son facile accommodement avec le mensonge." (*Lettres*, p. 56.) This letter is addressed: " Au R. P. Victor Poucel, rédacteur aux *Etudes*, ' revue catholique *d'intérêt général.*' " (Italics added.)

[23] Cf. Gide's letter to Richard Heyd (June 1948) in *T. C.*, VI, 142-143.

[24] *Retouches à mon retour de l'U.R.S.S.*, p. 103.

and self-righteous; both are selfish and materialistic but maintain
a correct impression through their close association with " Monsieur
l'Abbé "; and both attempt to justify their beliefs and actions by
recourse to what Eveline calls the " point de vue général." [25] The
wives, Eveline and Laure, are both martyrs to their husband's deceit
and self-esteem. There is, as well, a tension between father and
child in each work: the dislike of Geneviève for the Robert of the
récit and that of Michel for the Robert of the play. But where,
in the *récit*, the conflict is more of a personality-clash (for *L'Ecole
des femmes* is essentially a character study throughout), the Michel-
Robert antagonism in *L'Intérêt général* has, rather, a social and
ideological basis wherein the play draws its depth and interest.
And we become aware here, too, of the evolution of Gide's thought
in the 1930's from moral to social considerations and of the growing
distaste for both capitalism and catholicism that forms the atmosphere of this play.

Michel, younger son of Robert and Laure Dormoy is, in the
best tradition of Gide's adolescents, a *révolté* from the family circle,
from, as he states it, " le mensonge . . . cette misère morale . . .
ce confort égoïste que mes parents prennent pour du bonheur." [26]
Gustave, the older son (like his counterpart in the *Enfant prodigue*)
is firmly rooted in the " milieu familial." He seems to exist only
to emulate the clever, conniving ways of his devoted father. Laure,
the wife, sincere and well-meaning, secretly approves of Michel's
reproach of his father, but is too cowed by years of subjugation to
assume an influential rôle in the family's destiny. She compensates,
as best she can, through charity and hospital work, for the cold,
impassive home life generated by Robert and Gustave. Unknown
to his father, Michel finds daily sanctuary at the home of Boris
Orlov, or " Oncle Boris," who has the misfortune of being the
illegitimate son of Robert's father and a Russian woman, now both
deceased. Boris, a chemist and inventor, lives in Spartan surroundings with his son Ivan (a " chef d'atelier " at Robert's factory
and a fanatical supporter of union rights) and his daughter, Véra,
with whom Michel is enamored. Other characters in the drama
are L'Abbé Tronchet whose favorite counsel: " Sauvons la face ! " [27]

[25] *L'Ecole des femmes* (nouv. éd., Gallimard, 1930), p. 47.
[26] *T. C.*, VI, 64.
[27] *Ibid.*, p. 19.

finds constant reassurance with the Robert-Gustave clique; Rabot, unscrupulous foreman at the Dormoy factory; and, finally, ineffectual and naïve Cousin Arthur whose brief appearances in the play provide an element of comic relief.

With the smug comment that: " l'intérêt général ne s'arrête pas aux accablements particuliers," [28] Robert, at the opening of the play, quickly abandons his mournful guise—called for by his father's funeral—and settles down gleefully to the business of making money at anybody's and everybody's expense. The first victim is poor, unsuspecting Cousin Arthur from whom Robert extracts a large sum of money with a view to exploiting a new and valuable chemical formula discovered by Boris Orlov. Nor is Robert's enthusiasm for the Orlov venture in any way dampened by news that the factory workers are planning a strike. The ' right,' he feels, is bound to prevail—with the aid of strong police forces— against the injustices of an ignorant and inferior proletariat.

In Act II, Robert presents Boris Orlov with his offer. However, it is Ivan, the son, who intervenes to prevent Robert's deception of the more gullible Boris and who, as delegate for the striking union, lashes out at the *patron* in these terms:

Monsieur Dormoy, vous devriez comprendre qu'on ne peut ruiner que les riches. Notre fortune à nous, c'est nos bras, c'est notre travail. Notre force est dans notre entente . . . Vous pourrez bien nous affamer pendant quelques jours; mais votre régime a vécu et notre victoire est au bout.[29]

Ivan is concerned only with the proletariat as a mass, only with collective action. He is therefore sceptical of Michel's support of the workers' cause and what he considers an individualist, emotional approach to the issue.

On Ivan's insistence, Michel returns home (we are in Act III) to find his mother in conference with the Abbé. " Plus de misère, c'est dire du même coup: plus de charité," says the Abbé by way of convincing Laure that her concern for the hardships of the working classes is unwarranted. " Si le propre d'une âme chrétienne est de chercher à soulager la misère," he argues, ". . . il est impie de prétendre la supprimer." [30] Michel then confronts the Abbé with that Biblical maxim so often quoted throughout Gide's work: " Qui veut sauver sa vie la perdra," and insists that the self-interest

[28] *Ibid.*, p. 15.   [29] *Ibid.*, p. 57.   [30] *Ibid.*, p. 79.

and hypocrisy of Robert's acts can find no justification or sanction anywhere in the Scriptures.

Rabot, jealous of Michael's affection for Véra, has meanwhile informed Robert of his son's close association with the Orlov family. The resulting interview between Robert and Michel provides the definitive break between the two and clarifies the opposite poles of their respective philosophies.

ROBERT: . . . Nous sommes les dépositaires responsables d'un grand passé de traditions et de culture . . . d'un passé . . . qui fait la gloire de la France et contre lequel doit venir se briser l'hydre de l'anarchie. C'est pour ce glorieux patrimoine que je lutte . . . *Tout homme qui possède se doit d'être conservateur.* Tu regardes ta montre?

MICHEL: Oui, je voudrais savoir si vous en avez pour longtemps. Parce que mes amis les grévistes m'attendent.[31]

Michel, ordered from the Dormoy home, returns to join the workers' camp only to learn from Véra of Ivan's personal animosity and of the workers' reluctance to accept the "fils du patron" in their ranks. Left now completely alone and distrusted by both factions, Michel is nonetheless determined to prove his loyalty to the union cause.

Act IV finds the factory area well policed and guarded against any outbreak of violence. Robert and Gustave have taken all precautions against "cette rébellion des éléments inférieurs" and have even instructed Rabot—to the latter's delight—that Michel is not to be spared should he attempt to force the strike beyond the stage of passive resistance. As usual, Robert produces both Biblical and social justifications for this attitude: "L'Evangile, Rabot, nous enseigne, lorsqu'un membre est pourri, à le couper pour le rejeter loin du corps." And again: "Eliminer les éléments tarés, c'est le premier devoir de l'Etat et de la famille." [32]

From the terrace of their home, Robert, Gustave and Laure see a group of *grévistes*, including Michel and the Orlov children, congregating outside the factory. Suddenly, as anticipated, Michel separates from the group and crosses the police line. Hysterically,

[31] *Ibid.,* pp. 87-88. Italics added.

[32] *Ibid.,* p. 112.

Robert's mania for rationalization and self-justification fits Gide's own definition of the "esprit faux": ". . . c'est celui qui éprouve le besoin de se persuader qu'il a raison de commettre tous les actes qu'il a besoin de commettre."—*Journal des Faux-Monnayeurs, O. C.,* XIII, 33.

Laure rushes out to stop him but to no avail, for Robert has locked
the garden gate separating his property from the factory area. It
is then that Rabot grabs a pistol from one of the guards, fires at
Michel and kills him. The enraged workmen take chase and corner
Rabot as he beats frantically on the Dormoy's gate. Gustave watches
cynically from the garden but refuses to open. A second shot is
fired—this time by Véra—and Rabot dies. Véra and Ivan are
arrested.

The last act finds Robert again, as in Act I, in the rôle of bereaved
and long-suffering family-man but his thoughts, as before, are
directed to more practical matters—specifically, to the question of
the Orlov formula. As for Laure, the shock of Michel's death has
finally revealed to her the lies and deceit of Robert.

. . . Robert ne trompe que les autres . . . Il ment. Il ment sans cesse.
C'est cela que ne supportait pas Michel. Rien de ce que dit mon mari
n'est sincère . . .

The old Abbé agrees he has noted " quelque exagération dans
certaines déclarations de Monsieur Dormoy," [33] but adds hopefully
that only God is in a position to judge the sincerity of mortal acts.

Orlov arrives to beg Robert's intervention on behalf of Véra, and
the scheming M. Dormoy is only too glad to enhance his position
by an act of charity. It is agreed that Véra will be freed—but only
in return for the formula of Boris Orlov. On hearing of Robert's
' magnanimous ' gesture, Laure regrets her earlier doubts of her
husband's sincerity and the play ends in the triumph of the *patron*
and, of course, to the complete satisfaction of the Abbé. The
curtain falls as Robert intones: " Monsieur l'Abbé, restez à
déjeuner, je vous prie! . . ." [34]

An earlier play, *Le Repas du lion* by François de Curel, had
treated this theme of labor-management relations but in a more
philosophic and less satiric manner than is evident in *L'Intérêt
général*. In Curel's play, the moral evolution of the central character, Jean de Miremont, from Christian orator to champion of
the working classes, takes precedence over the social question
involved; nor are the author's prejudices for or against any faction

[33] *T. C.*, VI, 125.

[34] *Ibid.*, p. 138. One recalls here a Journal entry for February 1932:
" Que la société capitaliste ait pu chercher appui dans le christianisme,
c'est une monstruosité dont le Christ n'est pas responsable; mais le clergé."
(p. 1118)

or group emphasized beyond broad generalizations on justice, freedom and the Christian brotherhood. While nothing is actually solved in the Gide play, the bitter, satiric indictment of capitalism and the sympathetic treatment of the working classes show Gide to be a supporter of socialist doctrines and an opponent of the industrialist aristocracy.   Such a clear-cut position escapes the reader of Curel's essentially non-thesis character study. Curel's Jean and Gide's Michel are both idealists and sentimentalists, but whereas Jean has the opportunity to effect reforms from within the capitalist fold, Michel must necessarily break completely with his aristocratic heritage and oppose capitalism from within the labor ranks. The result is that the social and economic conflict is more sharply defined in the Gide play and one is left with the impression that a wealthy and privileged aristocracy is as bent on the subjugation of the proletariat as is the proletariat on the weakening of the aristocracy. Curel's Georges Boussard most nearly approaches Robert as the cold, practical materialist but is much less a caricature of the industrial potentate than is Robert upon whom Gide has directed the main satire of his play.

To sum up, the industrial question, in Curel's play, serves as a sort of proving-ground for testing and developing the character of the main personage just as, in Corneille's theatre, questions of duelling, treason and religious persecution seem of less importance, as issues in themselves, than as challenges to the moral integrity and physical resources of the hero. In Gide's play, however, the social and industrial questions are very real and pertinent and are all the more accentuated by the presentation of the protagonists as personifications of the extreme and opposite issues of the controversy.

Perhaps the closest parallel to Gide's study of Robert and Michel can be found in the father-daughter relationship of Octave Mirbeau's play, Les Affaires sont les affaires. Just as Michel hated his father, the idealistic and charitable Germaine has only contempt for the wealth and power of Isidore Lechat, for his utter lack of moral principle and his maltreatment of the working classes. And she condemns her father (II, 5) in terms which sum up, as well, the business ethic of Gide's Robert: " Des rapts, des coups de bourse, des chantages, des escroqueries qu'il décore du nom d'affaires. . . . Voilà son histoire ! " Mme Lechat is as devoted to Germaine as is

Laure Dormoy to Michel, but she, too, has become weak and ineffectual through years of subservience to her husband's will. The concept of the church as a vast commercial empire with great political influence emerges more than once from the dialogue of the Mirbeau play just as it is implied, in *L'Intérêt général*, through Robert's close affiliation with the Abbé. Finally, as was the case in Gide's work, the last act of the Mirbeau play finds Isidore Lechat mourning the death of his son. And, with the valiance of a Robert, Isidore manages to overcome his grief sufficiently to conclude an important business deal before the final curtain falls.

Unfortunately, as the first version of the play has not been conserved, it is impossible, by comparison with the final product, exactly to determine the extent and significance of Gide's changes prompted by his renunciation of communism. Nevertheless, one thing would seem clear: that however firm his intentions, Gide did not succeed in pushing the social theme from the forefront of his work. However much he may have wished to concentrate plot and dialogue on the character study of his two main protagonists, Robert and Michel, one is more impressed by the clash of ideas, systems and ideologies represented by father and son, by the opposition of the capitalist and socialist viewpoints, than one is by the delineation of the individual characters as such. As late as 1943, Gide fears that the production of *L'Intérêt général* at an *avant-garde* theatre "risquerait de prendre une allure trop subversive." And while insisting he has aimed at transforming the play from social satire to " comédie de caractères," he confesses in somewhat of an understatement: ". . . je n'ai pu faire disparaître complètement toutes les traces de cette première intention, désastreuse." [35]

If Gide renounced support of Soviet communism, it would be wrong to conclude that he therefore became more tolerant of old-guard capitalism and Catholic conservatism. His biting reproach of both groups in this, his last play, shows that his anticlerical and anticonformist stand remained intact and that while his social philosophy had been purged of Russian communist affiliation, his personal faith in liberalism and social progress and his hatred of traditionalism remained essentially the same as they were before that disillusioning experience in the summer of 1936.

[35] *Journal, 1942-1949*, p. 192.

CHAPTER VII

THE ESTHETICIAN AND MORALIST

1. Gide's Theatre and his Drama Criticism

In 1913, on the eve of the founding of the Vieux-Colombier, Jacques Copeau stressed the need for a renaissance in French drama:

. ... partout veulerie, désordre, indiscipline, ignorance et sottise, dédain du créateur, haine de la beauté, une production de plus en plus folle et vaine, une critique de plus en plus consentante, un goût public de plus en plus égaré: voilà ce qui nous indigne et nous soulève.[1]

André Gide, who had been closely allied with Copeau on *L'Ermitage* and was to join him in founding the *Nouvelle Revue Française*, shared his bitter resentment of the non-artistic, naturalistic tendencies in the French theatre in the years preceding the First World War. Close on the heels of the bourgeois theatre of Augier and Dumas *fils* there had followed the naturalistic "tranche de vie" drama of Zola and then, as of 1887, the trend towards realism and episodism engendered by the school of André Antoine and the Théâtre Libre. The thesis play, linked to social and political problems, was the order of the day and its exponents: Brieux and Hervieu, the toast of public and critics. "Tout m'y paraît prévu, conventionnel, outré, fastidieux," Gide writes of his distaste for the theatre at that time.[2] And again: "Je ne vais pas souvent au théâtre; l'ennui que j'y goûte est souvent infini."[3]

It is, then, in opposition to the popular trend of French drama that Gide joined forces with Lugné-Poë, Jacques Copeau and others in an effort to promote an idealistic reaction to this realistic,

---

[1] "Un Essai de rénovation dramatique," *Critiques d'un autre temps*, pp. 233-234.

[2] *S. G. N. M.*, *O. C.*, X, 214.

[3] *Lettres à Angèle*, *O. C.*, III, 200.

bourgeois drama and to encourage a new respect for the purely literary qualities of the " théâtre non-joué." In his important lecture, " L'Evolution du théâtre " (1904), Gide recalls Racine's advice on the importance of viewing dramatic characters outside the direct perspective of everyday life. The " episodisme " and illusion of reality of the naturalistic theatre has, Gide argues, closed the gap between stage and spectator; the actor has dropped his mask and with it all that is universal, poetic and evocative in the work of art. Portrayal of character and emotion has been replaced by the exposition of ideas and theses prompted by the popular tastes of the moment. And he adds:

Mais la plupart du temps, c'est à ces préoccupations précisément que la pièce doit sa vogue; l'auteur qui n'y obéit pas, que la seule préoccupation d'art fait écrire, risque fort de n'être même pas représenté.[4]

And again, as he writes in 1914: " L'art dramatique ne doit pas chercher à donner l'illusion de la réalité . . . une pièce de théâtre, c'est une durée à animer." [5]

This belief that dramatic art demands a gulf between stage and spectator that can be bridged only by intelligence and perception is clearly a characteristic of Gide's own theatre wherein the ideas— more often veiled in symbol and abstraction than directly exposed— are seldom perceptible at first glance. What he writes, in 1924, of his intellectual approach to art would certainly seem to apply to the complexities and hidden meanings we have already observed in the plays prior to 1935: ". . . c'est . . . que j'ai plus grand souci de cacher ma pensée que de la dire, et qu'il me paraît plus séant de la laisser découvrir par qui la cherche vraiment, que de l'exposer." [6] In view of this attitude, it is not difficult to appreciate his distaste for such plays as Hauptmann's *The Weavers* or Renard's *La Bigote*, as for all plays where interpretation and artistry are sacrificed to the exposition of a social or religious thesis.

The intense effort demanded by Gide of his readers and interpreters precludes a popular enthusiasm for many of his plays where the meaning—sometimes obscure in reading—is often lost completely in the rapid dialogue of stage presentation.

[4] *O. C.*, IV, 203.
[5] *Journal*, p. 423.
[6] " Lettre à André Rouveyre " (31 oct. 1924), *Lettres*, p. 27.

L'on pourrait dire qu'il y a deux sortes d'attentions: l'une intense, l'autre à demi distraite et discursive. . . .

....

C'est pour ne compter point sur cette attention prolongée, la seconde, que je fais appel à la première, l'attention intense, infiniment plus rare, plus difficile à obtenir et plus chichement accordée. . . .[7]

Gide's principal criticism of the modern French theatre is, then, its concentration on present-day realities and its concern for questions and problems incidental and external to the basic character of man. The dramatist should be the guide not the slave of popular morality and must present new examples of grandeur and heroism, new ideals for the liberation and development of the individual.

Que de héros cachés, qui n'attendent que l'exemple du héros d'un livre, qu'une étincelle de vie pour vivre, que sa parole pour parler. N'est-ce pas là ... ce que nous espérons également du théâtre? Qu'il propose à l'humanité de nouvelles formes d'héroïsme, de nouvelles figures de héros.[8]

Contemporary society, he feels, allows only one form of heroism: that of resignation and acceptance. Only with a separation of actor from spectator, of reality from fiction and of the hero from the mantle of contemporary morals will a dramatic renaissance be possible. Gide believes that Ibsen condemns his heroes to moral bankruptcy by confining them to the limits of modern bourgeois ethics. He finds stress on fatal passion in Racine's theatre a weakening rather than an exalting factor in character development. The love-theme in Corneille, however,—more idealistic and estimable—"obtient de chacun le plus noble, le meilleur."[9] This moral idealism dominates Gide's theatre, each play depicting the attempts of the hero to advance beyond the anarchy of the self and the present towards something greater and more permanent. The outward follies and weaknesses of a Saül or a Candaule are, to Gide, of little value in themselves unless considered as manifestations of an inner unrest and dissatisfaction which the would-be 'hero' must overcome. In 1931—the year when his chef-d'oeuvre of heroism, *Oedipe*, was produced—Gide writes:

[7] *Journal*, pp. 690-691.
[8] "L'Evolution du théâtre," *O. C.*, IV, 216.
[9] *Journal, 1939-1942*, p. 103.

Les faiblesses, les abandons, les déchéances de l'homme, nous les connais-
sons de reste et la littérature de nos jours n'est que trop habile à les
dénoncer; mais ce surpassement de soi qu'obtient la volonté tendue, c'est
là ce que nous avons surtout besoin qu'on nous montre.[10]

Gide's is clearly a theatre of ideas—but the ideas are not, as in
the conventional thesis play, restricted to external phenomena.
They are rather functions of the character and temperament of
the individual protagonist. And the ideas of the individual protagonists represent, as we have already seen, successive stages in
the development of Gide's own inner dialogue. When Prométhée,
referring to his eagle, remarks paradoxically: " Je n'aime pas les
hommes; j'aime ce qui les dévore," [11] he means, as does Gide, that
his concern is not with the surface aspects of man but rather with
the ideas, motivations and essence of the individual. Gide writes,
in 1924, of this neglect of objective reality for the study and
evaluation of the moral conflict:

Je puis dire que ce n'est pas à moi-même que je m'intéressai, mais au
conflit de certaines idées dont mon âme n'était que le théâtre et où je
faisais fonction moins d'acteur que de spectateur, de témoin.[12]

If man's struggle for moral perfection is proposed by Gide as
a more worthwhile concern of the drama than the exposition of
social theses and " tranches de vie," how can one explain the
absence of moral analysis and the social and religious satire of
his last two plays? To attribute this esthetic ' betrayal ' alone to
an emotional and abortive alliance with communism would be too
simple—although his affiliation with that group undoubtedly in-
fluenced the extent and enthusiasm of his commitment. Gide's
interest in the social welfare of mankind, carried beyond the earlier
stage of concern solely for the moral welfare of the individual, is
consistent with that idealistic side of his nature to which we have
referred. The presentation of objective and actual issues seems
inconsistent, however, with what we have seen of his earlier dramatic
esthetic. The naturalistic tradition of the Théâtre Libre which
had, many years before, prompted Gide's association with an
idealistic reaction, had long since been eclipsed by a more poetic

[10] " Préface à Vol de nuit," Feuillets d'automne, p. 210.
[11] Le Prométhée mal enchaîné, O. C., III, 130.
[12] Journal, p. 783.

7

and literary theatre. This fact alone might morally justify his momentary departure from the classical tradition with *L'Intérêt général* and *Le Treizième Arbre*. More fundamental, however, is the fact that Gide's psychic conflict—which we have observed in the plays from *Saül* to *Oedipe*—had, by 1930, been largely resolved and the stage cleared for the more realistic, non-moral observations of these last two plays. But, as has been said, this departure *was*, it seems, only temporary. Gide subsequently regretted the emphasis on realism of *L'Intérêt général* and his writings from 1940 to the time of his death show again a return to predominantly literary, esthetic concerns (*i. e., Interviews imaginaires, Attendu que . . . , Thésée, Feuillets d'automne, Ainsi soit-il*).

Just as realism and objectivism had deprived the theatre of heroic figures so, too, they endangered the concept of morality as an individual and subjective problem.[13]

> Le danger de la foule, hélas! c'est aussi qu'elle a faim. Elle demande qu'on la nourrisse. . . . On invente la pièce à thèse. C'est un aliment creux. Qu'importe! si la foule s'en satisfait.[14]

As for the " vrais nourrisseurs," the enemies of mediocrity and conformity, they must learn to ignore the public, " tout au moins *l'attendre,* en répétant avec Stendhal, Nietzsche et tant d'autres: ceux qui me comprendront ne sont pas encore nés." [15]

The public's demand for moral conformity is further assuaged, Gide believes, by the advocates of Christian drama. Yet, he argues, ' drama ' implies ' character ' but Christianity is opposed to character by proposing a common ideal and ethic for each individual. A *Saint-Genest* or a *Polyeucte* are Christian, yes, but are dramas only because of the non-Christian element which the Christian element combats. Monotheism implies a regulation and one-sidedness which is foreign to the basic, complex nature of man and which restrains his full and natural evolution.[16] " . . . Qu'on nous redonne

---

[13] Gide's criticism of the popular influence on literature reminds one of a similar condemnation by Stendhal in 1836 when, as he writes, taste was generally approaching the " médiocrité grossière qui est le despote, et à laquelle il faut faire la cour. . . ." Cf. *Mélanges de littérature,* III, 430 ff. (Paris, Le Divan, 1933).

[14] " De l'Importance du public," *O. C.,* IV, 195.

[15] *Ibid.,* p. 196 note.

[16] *Ibid.,* pp. 191-192: " Aucun art n'a pu être enfanté par le monothéisme

la liberté des moeurs, et la contrainte de l'art suivra; qu'on supprime
l'hypocrisie et le masque remontera sur la scène." [17] The weakness
of an authoritarian moral code is illustrated, in Gide's theatre, in
the subjection of Saül and David before religious authority and
superstition and in their inability to solve the psychic conflict
independently and subjectively. The champions of individualism
and " dénûment " are, on the other hand, the pagan heroes Oedipe
and Philoctète, whose independence of the deity leads not to
passivity and self-indulgence, but to moral harmony and well-being.
The Christian element, it is true, has a symbolic rôle in Gide's
Enfant prodigue but there it is a personal, humanistic Christ—
stripped of dogma and superstition—who is the advocate not of
convention and conformity but of emancipation and individualism.

Only independence of public demands and social pressure can
assure sincerity in the work of art: this is, in sum, the dramatic
esthetic of Gide and one which is consistently observed in his
writings. The psychological insight and the subjectivity of his
plays owe much to this stand against commercial and popular
inroads on his art. His approach to the theatre has been well
defined by these words, previously quoted, of his hero Philoctète:
" Je m'exprime mieux depuis que je ne parle plus à des hommes.
. . . Je compris que les mots sont plus beaux dès qu'ils ne servent
plus aux demandes." [18] Nor was this faith in individual expression
compromised in any way by Gide's espousal of socialist views
when, some thirty-eight years after the composition of *Philoctète*,
he repeats the same view in much the same terms:

On parle fort bien dans le désert, alors qu'aucun écho ne risque de déformer
le son de la voix; alors qu'on n'a pas à se préoccuper du retentissement
de ses paroles *et que rien d'autre ne les incline qu'un souci de sincérité.*[19]

2. The Interdependence of Morality and Esthetics

Gide recalls in his memoirs his attitude of mind in 1893 just
before the African trip and his revolt from the moral restraints
of Puritanism and the esthetic escapism of the symbolist period:

. . . et, pour que le christianisme pût à neuf imager la terre, il fallut que
l'informe dieu des prophètes descendît en l'homme s'incarner."

[17] " L'Evolution du théâtre," *O. C.*, IV, 215.

[18] *T. C.*, I, 161.

[19] " Discours aux étudiants de Moscou," *Littérature engagée*, p. 137.
Italics added.

. . . nous nous poussions, je me souviens, vers un idéal d'équilibre, de plénitude et de santé. Ce fut, je crois bien, ma première orientation vers ce qu'on appelle aujourd'hui ' le classicisme.' [20]

This serenity, order and harmony which classicism implies remained, as we have seen through the psychological revelations of his theatre, the main goal of Gide's efforts as a moral philosopher. But can it be said that he envisaged and achieved this same classic balance on an esthetic plane? If Gide's writings avoid the extremes of both romanticism and naturalism, what, if anything, do his plays reveal of his qualities as a classic writer?

The Biblical and Greek inspiration of his theatre follows in the French classical tradition but his subjective reinterpretation of these ancient themes in terms of their moral and psychological significance has provided characters and problems of a depth and complexity far distant from the more simple, uncomplicated psychology of his seventeenth-century predecessors.[21] In brief, Gide has made almost exclusive use of classical themes in his theatre but in so doing has replaced the universal Man of Corneille and Racine by more individual and specific cases; he has refined and extended the elementary motives of love, hate and passion by analyzing such questions as homosexuality, narcissism and sensualism which, in Boileau's day, would undoubtedly have constituted a breach with *vraisemblance* and the *bienséances*. Yet again he has departed from the Greek tradition by denying the rôles of fate and predestination and by making his protagonists the sole arbiters of their own destiny. Of the three unities, only unity of action is observed [22] (*Candaule* and *Oedipe* have three acts rather than five; *Bethsabé* has only three scenes and there are but three lines to the last act of *Philoctète*). With a view to emphasizing the psychological conflict, Gide does, however, adhere to the Racinian principle of eliminating lengthy expositions, suppressing incidental characters and avoiding secondary plots. In all, Gide's theatre

---

[20] *S. G. N. M., O. C.*, X, 350.

[21] Gide's transformation and humanization of Old Testament history, Christian parable and Greek legend has set a precedent for such neo-Hellenic dramatists as Giraudoux, Cocteau, Anouilh and Sartre who, while less subjective and self-analytical in their methods, have, like Gide, lent a modern philosophic or psychological slant to the myth.

[22] For Gide and the unities, see Hytier, *André Gide*, p. 203.

reveals much that is new and unconventional and it is obvious that he has taken many liberties with his classical sources. But must it therefore be said that individualism and classicism are mutually exclusive? Not so in Gide's case; for just as he has approached the moral problem independent of an imposed, *a priori* ethic, so too, by extension and analogy, the order and discipline of his art is subjective and self-imposed. As he himself states it:

Il me semble que *les qualités* . . . *classiques sont surtout des qualités morales*, et volontiers je considère le classicisme comme un harmonieux faisceau de vertus, dont la première est la modestie. Le romantisme est toujours accompagné d'orgueil, d'infatuation. *La perfection classique implique, non point certes une suppression de l'individu (. . .) mais la soumission de l'individu, sa subordination, et celle du mot dans la phrase*, de la phrase dans la page, de la page dans l'oeuvre.[23]

Morality and esthetics are interdependent with Gide, and the form and the content of his writings, the emotion and the expression of the emotion are inseparable. This will be found to be particularly true of his theatre where the outward expression is so closely bound to the inner emotions of the author. It is the desire for harmony in the inner dialogue which, in turn, promotes the desire for creative art. This externalization of an emotion in literary form is impossible, however, without a prior urge to bring order and discipline to the conflict of moral extremes.

. . . l'amour du désordre est incapable de produire une oeuvre d'art; mes livres sont là pour le prouver. Si tout mon être ne tendait pas à l'ordre et à l'harmonie, je n'aurais jamais pu les écrire, et je n'en aurais pas eu le désir.[24]

Each of Gide's plays corresponds to such inner motivation and promotes, through its catharsis of disturbing emotions and tendencies, a greater integration of the personality.

If, then, the moralist must depend on self-criticism and effort to attain an eventual " dénûment " and " dépassement," these same qualities are no less important to the classicist who aims at order and discipline in the work of art; the renunciation and discipline

[23] " Réponse à une enquête . . . sur le classicisme," *O. C.*, X, 25-26. Italics added.

[24] " Lettre à André Rouveyre " (10 nov. 1924), *Lettres*, p. 35.

required by classicism are implicit in the moral triumph of individualism through the renunciation of individuality.

Le triomphe de l'individualisme et le triomphe du classicisme se confondent. Or le triomphe de l'individualisme est dans le renoncement à l'individualité. Il n'est pas une des qualités du style classique qui ne s'achète pas par le sacrifice d'une complaisance. . . . L'oeuvre classique ne sera forte et belle qu'en raison de son romantisme dompté.[25]

This interdependence of the moral and the esthetic has been illustrated by Gide in his *Philoctète* where the hero remarks to Ulysse: "Je voudrais mes actions plus solides et plus belles; vraies, pures, cristallines. . . ."[26] Later, with the free and independent sacrifice of his possessions to the Greeks, there follows on this moral victory a state of esthetic perfection: "Sa voix est devenue extraordinairement belle et douce. . . ."[27] The experience of Philoctète is, in sum, Gide's own struggle to evolve both an order and sincerity in his art and a harmony and gratuity of the inner being. And it is as much the experience of the classic writer as of the moral philosopher. As Gide affirms in his *Journal*:

Il m'est bien difficile de croire que la pensée la plus saine, la plus sage et la plus sensée ne soit pas aussi celle qui, projetée dans l'écriture, donne les lignes les plus harmonieuses et les plus belles.[28]

[25] *Billets à Angèle*, *O. C.*, XI, 36.
[26] *T. C.*, I, 163.
[27] *Ibid.*, p. 180.
[28] *Journal* (1928), p. 889.

Chapter VIII

CONCLUSION

Gide believes there are two methods of portraying life in literature: the first, external and objective, observes, explains and inter-
prets the outward gestures and manifestations of reality; the
second, concerned more with emotion and thought, invents circum-
stances and characters best suited to the illustration and interpretation of these values. The second method, which Gide adopts, is
largely dependent, however, on a prior experience by the author
of the emotional life it depicts.

La richesse de celui-ci [l'auteur], sa complexité, l'antagonisme de ses
possibilités trop diverses, permettront la plus grande diversité de ses
créations. Mais c'est de lui que tout émane. Il est le seul garant de la
vérité qu'il révèle, le seul juge. *L'enfer et le ciel de ses personnages sont
en lui. Ce n'est pas lui qu'il peint; mais ce qu'il peint il aurait pu le
devenir s'il n'était pas devenu tout lui-même. . . .*[1]

This, indeed, is the psychological method of Gide's theatre wherein
the moral problem is studied through the medium of Gide's own
emotions and experience, each of his characters embodying or
symbolizing a tendency of an inner dialectic of moral extremes. The
cathartic effect of this externalization of the inner conflict in
dramatic form is apparent in the parallel development of Gide
himself and of his protagonists from the unbalanced ethic of a
Saül or a Candaule to the integrated individualism of an Oedipe.
The ideal of self-fulfilment, first presented in *Philoctète*, is actually
attained only when the many and contrasting psychological tensions
have been liberated and put to the test. By giving life and expression, through his protagonists, to these varied facets of his personality—rather than burying them in the depths of the subconscious—
Gide succeeds in preserving the completeness and authenticity of
his nature. In the passivity of Saül, the irrationalism of Candaule

---

[1] *Un Esprit non prévenu,* pp. 38-39. Italics added.

and the illusionism of David, he depicts the dangers of subjecting
the personality to the domination of any single psychological
extreme. Consequently, he is better able to control these natural
instincts and promote a balance between the satanic and the
Puritanical elements of the inner dialogue. What Gide says of
Dostoyevsky's relation to his characters is particularly true of his
own association with Saül, David, Candaule or Oedipe: " Il vit
en chacun d'eux, et cet abandon de soi dans leur diversité a pour
premier effet de protéger ses propres inconséquences." [2] Nowhere
in Gide's writings can this subjective, psychological approach be
better observed than in the plays which, devoid as they are of
external pressure and esthetic compromise, remain a faithful reflection of the inner drama and moral evolution of their author.

Each great moral reform, Gide has said, has at its origin a
physical or mental disturbance, an emotional conflict or uncertainty.[3] That this is true of his theatre we have attempted to show
through the identification of the succeeding phases of his moral
philosophy with the motivations, ideas and actions of his protagonists. Each play and each character represents a step forward in
the moral development of its author—in the evolution, through
self-criticism and analysis, from the illusions and disorders of
Saül and Candaule to the balanced, harmonious ethic of Oedipe.

In considering the significance of Gide's theatre in the light of
his moral evolution we have continually stressed the idealism, the
self-searching and the psychological emphasis of the plays. Gide,
as a critic, has sought out and admired these same human qualities
in such writers as Montaigne, Goethe, Baudelaire and Dostoyevsky
and established them as a sort of *sine qua non* of intellectual and
artistic integrity. " Seul l'art m'agrée, parti de l'inquiétude, qui
tende à la sérénité," he writes.[4] Can it not be said that this credo
finds its fullest and most complete manifestation in the moral
revelations of his theatre?

---

[2] *Conférences sur Dostoïevsky, O. C.*, XI, 161.
[3] *Ibid.*, p. 292.
[4] *Journal, 1939-1942*, p. 87.

APPENDICES

I. NOTES ON THE STAGE PRODUCTION
OF GIDE'S PLAYS

(The plays are treated in the order of their production for the stage.
The date in brackets is that of the first presentation. *Le Retour, Bethsabé,
Ajax* and *Proserpine* have not yet been produced.)

1. *Le Roi Candaule (1901)*

The first presentation was given by "L'Oeuvre" under the
direction of Lugné-Poë at the Nouveau Théâtre in Paris on May 9,
1901. Lugné-Poë, Edouard de Max and Henrietta Roggers played
the rôles of Candaule, Gygès and Nyssia, respectively. The most
recent *reprise* of the play was presented in May-June, 1949, at the
Théâtre du Pavillon de France, in Paris, with Jean Lanier (Candaule), Jacques Mafioly (Gygès) and Claire Jordan (Nyssia).

Press reaction to the first production was almost uniformly
unfavorable or indifferent. Gide himself has collected a long list
of these critical comments as part of his "Préface de la seconde
édition" (cf. *T. C.*, II, 35 ff.) to inform the reader, as he says
ironically, "sur l'excellence de la critique dramatique dans les
journaux de l'an 1901."

Emile Faguet:
> Je regrette qu'elle [la pièce] soit écrite dans cet idiome rythmique
> si bizarre qui est à mi-chemin de la prose et des vers. . . .
> —"Feuilleton" du *Journal des Débats* (13 mai 1901).

Gustave Larroumet:
> [*Le Roi Candaule*] m'a intéressé à la lecture et ennuyé à la repré-
> sentation. —"Feuilleton" du *Temps* (13 mai 1901).

Catulle Mendès:
> Je dirais peut-être,—si la préface de M. Gide ne m'interdisait toute
> appréciation, qu'il y a, avec quelque ridicule dans la réalisation
> scénique, un peu de grandeur . . . et même une beauté, dans le rêve
> vaincu du pauvre roi Candaule. —*Le Journal* (9 mai 1901).

Henri Fouquier:

> M. Gide nous d̶i̶t̶ qu'il a voulu faire oeuvre d'art simplement! Mais quelle oeuvre dramatique n'a pas cette visée? . . . Je n'y entends rien. —*Le Figaro* (9 mai 1901).

And Gide gives us the general tone of the German reaction to his *Candaule* (presented at Berlin, January 8, 1908) in this quotation from *Bühne und Welt* comparing the Gide and Hebbel versions (cf. *Journal*, p. 262).

> 'Hebbels Auffassung steht für unser Empfinden ebenso hoch über der Gides, wie etwa Kleists Ausgestaltung des Amphytryons Stoffes über der Molières.'

2. Philoctète (1919)

Philoctète was first presented at a private theatre in Paris on April 3, 1919, with Arnold Naville, Jacques Naville and Pierre Naville in the rôles of Philoctète, Néoptolème and Ulysse, respectively. On October 16, 1937, during the " manifestations littéraires " of the Exposition Internationale de Paris, a reading of *Philoctète* was given at the Comédie des Champs-Elysées by Marcel Herrand and Jean Marchat of the Rideau de Paris. Press commentary has not been available on these two performances.

A third production of *Philoctète*—and a most unusual and interesting one (of which no mention has been made by Gide's bibliographers and editors)—took the form of a " lecture imagée " of the play given by the group " Art et Action " on January 8, 1921, at the inauguration of the Théâtre de Chambre. A large translucent screen representing the figures of Philoctète, Néoptolème and Ulysse was placed on the stage and each portrait was illuminated in turn as Mme Lara and Armand Bour interpreted the rôles of the three protagonists. A description of this unique presentation is found in *La Revue de l'Epoque* (no. 14, fév. 1921, p. 542):

> A chaque réplique, sur l'écran représentant les stylisations de M. Klein, s'allumaient des ampoules invisibles qui éclairaient seulement le personnage en train de parler. . . . Telle était la traduction synthétique des rôles sur l'écran coloré que, à chaque fois, Néoptolème, Ulysse et Philoctète paraissaient vraiment donner la réplique. Lara et Armand Bour, dans l'ombre . . . donnèrent une âme lumineuse au texte.

3. Saül (1922)

In dedicating *Saül* to Edouard de Max, Gide had hoped to see the famous actor in the title rôle and contemplated a production of the play—soon after its publication—at the Théâtre Antoine. "Je suis heureux de vous dire que de Max accepte—et avec joie, le rôle," Gide writes Raymond Bonheur in April 1904 (cf. *Le Retour*, 1st. ed., p. 86). However, this project failed, and *Saül* was not produced until 1922, some twenty-five years after Gide had begun its composition. The first of ten presentations took place on June 16, 1922 at the Théâtre du Vieux Colombier with Jacques Copeau as *metteur en scène* and music by Arthur Honegger. The cast of this first production included: Jacques Copeau (Saül), Carmen d'Assilva (La Reine), Pierre Daltour (David), François Vibert (Jonathan), Louis Jouvet (Le Grand Prêtre), and Blanche Albane (La Sorcière d'Endor).

Critical reaction was evenly divided between the merits and demerits of the play. More than one critic found *Saül's* qualities "plus livresques que dramatiques." A cross-section of press criticism follows:

Gaston Rageot:
> ... l'on y retrouve toutes les complications spirituelles ou autres qui, il y a vingt ans, dirigeaient l'inspiration d'André Gide.
> —*Revue Politique et Littéraire* (1 juillet 1922).

Pierre Brisson:
> L'ensemble manque de mouvement, de pathétique et de grandeur. Aucune figure n'est marquée de traits décisifs. . . . On dirait d'un jeu d'esprit, un conte sur le mode sérieux et sans les grâces de l'ironie.
> —"Feuilleton" du *Temps* (26 juin 1922).

Georges Bourdon:
> Mais quelle force sobre et vraiment classique dans toute l'oeuvre! Quelle hardiesse dans la coupe des scènes et dans le dialogue varié.
> —*Comoedia* (18 juin 1922).

Paul Granet:
> ... à la représentation, son drame nous déçoit et nous déconcerte ... par cet alliage de grandiloquence pathétique et de raffinement précieux. . . . Ce n'est ni un triomphe ni un échec.
> —*Europe Nouvelle* (1 juillet 1922).

4. *Le Retour de l'enfant prodigue (1928)*

The first French production was given by the Théâtre du Rideau (Marcel Herrand, director) on December 4, 1928, at the Théâtre de Monte-Carlo. The Paris *première*, again by the Compagnie du Rideau, was on February 23, 1933, at the Théâtre de l'Avenue. Marcel Herrand directed the production which, according to *Comoedia* (23 fév. '33), was staged "devant des rideaux et sans décors pour laisser au texte toute sa valeur." The text was read, not memorized. Music by Henri Sauguet separated the four tableaux comprising the dialogues of the Prodigue with the four members of his family. Included in the cast were: Léon Gautier (Le Lecteur), Marcel Herrand (Le Prodigue), Guy Favières (Le Père), Germaine Geranne (La Mère), Jean Dasté (L'Aîné) and François Jean (Le Puîné).

It is interesting to note that Jean-Louis Barrault played the Enfant Puîné in a *reprise* of the play by Le Rideau de Paris on June 18, 1934, at the Atelier. Yet another production by Marcel Herrand and Jean Marchat, in June 1939, is noteworthy in that the single "lecteur" of the previous productions was replaced by a group of "lecteurs"—adolescents dressed as campers or scouts, each of whom introduced a tableau which was then acted out at the other side of the stage.

Marcel Herrand offers some valuable comments in an interview with Henri Philippon before the 1933 production:

Quant au *Retour de l'enfant prodigue*, c'est une oeuvre qui est extrêmement connue à l'étranger, où elle est jouée en particulier en Suède et en Allemagne. Vous n'ignorez pas qu'elle est étudiée dans toutes les écoles allemandes comme texte classique français. Et cependant, à Paris, elle n'a pas encore été jouée par un théâtre régulier. M. Lugné-Poë avait l'intention de la donner au théâtre de l'Oeuvre, et c'est avec son autorisation que je pourrai la monter dans quelques jours.

—*L'Intransigeant* (12 fév. 1933).

The following comments are representative of the generally favorable reaction to the 1933 production:

Etienne Roy:

Ce n'est pas du théâtre, dira-t-on. Qu'importe? Ils [les tableaux] supportent fort bien la representation, même sans décors, car seuls comptent le texte, la pensée et la forme.

—*Comoedia* (26 fév. 1933).

Lugné-Poë:

La beauté intégrale des images qu'a dialoguées André Gide est aussi émouvante et d'une poésie plus ardente que celle de Renard dans *Poil de carotte*. —*Avenir* (4 mars 1933).

Edouard Bourdet:

Jamais la lumineuse et harmonieuse précision du texte de M. André Gide ne parut aussi savoureuse qu'après l'orageuse complication de la pièce de Strindberg. —*Marianne* (1 mars 1933).

(On the same program with Gide's play was Tage Aurell's translation: *La Plus Forte* of Strindberg.)

5. *Oedipe (1931)*

Oedipe was first produced by the Compagnie Pitoëff on December 10, 1931, at the ' Cercle Artistique " of Antwerp, and performances followed at Brussels (Dec. 18, '31), Geneva (Jan. 28, '32), Lausanne (Feb. 5) and Montreux (Feb. 6). The Paris *première,* directed and with costumes and *décors* by Georges Pitoëff, took place on February 18, 1932, at the Théâtre de l'Avenue. Members of the cast were: Georges Pitoëff (Oedipe), Jean Hort (Tirésias), Henri Gaultier (Créon), Jean Riveyre (Etéocle), Raymond Dagaud (Polynice), Nora Sylvère (Jocaste), Ludmilla Pitoëff (Antigone) and Eve Casalis (Ismène).

The press reaction to *Oedipe* was either unfavorable or indifferent. Excepting a very laudatory review by Lugné-Poë in *Avenir* (20 fév. '32), most critics found Gide's play essentially undramatic and objected to the modernisms of style, the puns and " jeux de mots " and the *mélange* of comic and tragic elements. (In a preface to the play—written especially for the Antwerp public—Gide had said: ". . . le bouffon s'y mêle étroitement au tragique. J'espère émouvoir, mais serais bien déçu si . . . l'on n'y rit." Gide was annoyed (cf. *Journal*, p. 1129) when this notice—intended only to reassure the public " un peu lourd " of Antwerp, and where he seems to attach undue importance to the humor of the play—was reproduced, without his permission, on the Paris program of the Compagnie Pitoëff.)

James de Coquet:
> . . . M. André Gide a eu raison de nous avertir que . . . le bouffon se mêlerait au tragique. Seulement, son tragique n'est peut-être pas aussi intense qu'il l'avait cru. Et cela tient à ce qu'il nous présente d'abord le personnage d'Oedipe sous les dehors les plus bourgeois.
> —*Le Figaro* (21 fév. 1932).

Etienne Rey:
> . . . je préfère l'Oedipe sérieux à l'Oedipe qui blague, et qui veut être ' moderne ' dans son langage. —*Comoedia* (20 fév. 1932).

Pierre Brisson:
> La pièce est à lire et constitue un jeu d'esprit.
> —" Feuilleton " du *Temps* (22 fév. 1933).

Lucien Dubech:
> C'est un auteur important qui n'est pas un auteur populaire. . . .

> Ce n'est pas un homme de théâtre. Il est de ceux qu'on peut appeler
> les livresques, les intellectuels tout purs.
>
> —*Candide* (25 fév. 1933).

François Porché:

> Un texte gidien en proie à l'acteur, à la vocifération, à la grimace,
> est bientôt déchiré. . . . Il disparaît entièrement et nous ne voyons
> plus que le comédien qui s'acharne à détruire ce qu'il croit exprimer.
>
> —*Revue de Paris* (15 mars 1932, p. 448).

More favorable comment greeted a *reprise* of *Oedipe* on July 21,
1949, when the play was presented by Jean Vilar and his group
(on a program with Montherlant's *Pasiphaé*) at the Festival
d'Avignon:

> En quelque endroit de son *Journal* Gide affirme qu'il n'écrivit jamais rien
> de bon que dans la joie. . . . Son *Oedipe* fut certainement créé dans la
> joie. On éprouvait à l'entendre un plaisir très vif.
>
> —Henry Magnan in *Le Monde* (23 juillet 1949).

> . . . c'est bien une créature d'André Gide que Vilar a choisi de nous
> montrer ce soir. L'ironie qui enchantait si bien la lecture est revenue
> vivre ici.   —J.-B. Jeener in *Le Figaro* (23 juillet 1949).

The Vilar Company presented *Oedipe* in Paris at the Marigny
theatre on April 4, 1951.

6. *Perséphone (1934)*

The first performance was at the Opéra de Paris on April 30,
1934, by the Ballets de Mme Ida Rubinstein with music by Igor
Stravinsky. Jacques Copeau directed the *mise en scène*, choreography was by Kurt Joos, and André Barsacq created the *décors*
and costumes. The work was presented in three tableaux: " Perséphone ravie," " Perséphone aux Enfers " and " Perséphone renais-
sante," and was interpreted through the triple medium of dance,
chorus and spoken dialogue. Included in the cast were: Ida
Rubinstein (Perséphone), Anatole Wiltzak (Mercure), René Maison
(Eumolpe), Mme Krasovska (Déméter) and M. Lester (Triptolème). On November 28, 1934, the same company presented
Perséphone at Queen's Hall, London.

In a newspaper article prior to the Paris production, Ida Rubinstein discussed the Gide-Stravinsky humanization of the myth and
her collaboration with them to create a synthesis of poetry, music
and dance:

> *Perséphone* . . . a été inspirée à Igor Stravinsky et à André Gide par

l'hymne homérique de Déméter, mais le maître musicien et André Gide ont transfiguré le mythe grec. Leur Perséphone est la première missionnaire, elle n'est pas ravie par Pluton, elle descend aux Enfers de son plein gré, c'est-à-dire qu'elle s'en va vers l'humanité souffrante.

Si la danse, engendrée par la musique et couronnée de poésie, ne craint pas de dérouler une action . . . c'est le spectacle complet, celui dont le langage est capable d'émouvoir le plus. Je crois à cette forme de l'art, à sa noblesse, à sa puissance. Je m'efforce, avec mes collaborateurs, de lui donner sa plus haute signification humaine.

—*Excelsior* (10 déc. 1933).

The critics' reaction to this " spectacle complet " was generally favorable although not enthusiastic:

Robert Brussel:
> . . . l'interprétation de M. André Gide est plus musicale, plus lyrique surtout que n'eût été une version plus respectueuse des traditions.
> —*Le Figaro* (8 mai 1934).

Henry Malherbe (referring to Gide's transformation of the myth):
> Par ses soins, le mythe s'est coloré au souffle du christianisme. Le sentiment de la souffrance humaine, à peu près inconnu dans l'antiquité, plane sur tout le drame.
> —" Feuilleton " du *Temps* (9 mai 1934).

An anonymous critic has this to say:
> ' Mon terrestre époux . . . Retour du printemps . . . Grenade mordue . . . Un peu d'amour . . .' On dirait des titres de chansons pour Lucienne Boyer. Ah comme nous aimions Gide quand il écrivait les *Caves du Vatican!* —*Paris-Midi* (1 mai 1934).

7. *Le Treizième Arbre (1935)*

The first performance was given at Marseilles on May 8, 1935, by the Rideau Gris—" club théâtral d'avant-garde "—on whose program (5ᵉ année, 24ᵉ spectacle) we read: " André Gide en composant le *Treizième Arbre* s'est, pour la première fois, volontairement plié à toutes les règles du théâtre."

The Paris *première* was given on January 13, 1939 by the Rideau de Paris at the Théâtre Charles de Rochefort. The production was directed by Marcel Herrand and the cast included: Jean Marchat (Le Docteur), Charles Nissar (Le Philologue), Charlotte Clasis (La Comtesse), Jean Bonvilliers (Le Curé) and Max de Guy (Le Vicomte).

The critics found the play entertaining and well-suited for the stage. (The humor was doubtless heightened by the appearance of Gide's farce on the same program with Lorca's *Noces de sang*.)

Georges le Cardonnel:

C'est bien la première fois que M. André Gide aura réussi à faire rire. Sa petite comédie fait penser . . . au meilleur Anatole France. Elle est amusante et quel plaisir d'entendre au théâtre une belle langue!   —*Le Journal* (16 janvier 1939).

Edmond Sée:

Il nous donne ici, après Sacha Guitry, la 'comédie de la psychanalyse,' une gentille satire des théories freudistes sur le refoulement.   —*Oeuvre* (20 janvier 1939).

Antoine:

. . . cette pièce mériterait de faire une carrière, et aurait pu trouver sa place dans le répertoire de la Comédie-Française. C'est une sorte de satire que l'auteur modestement avait qualifiée farce, en réalité une comédie de grand style.   —*L'Information* (21 janvier 1939).

8. *Robert ou l'Intérêt général (1946)*

The first performance was given by the amateur group " L'Essor " ("théâtre pour tous") at the Théâtre Municipal de Tunis on April 30, 1946. The production was directed by Alexandre Fichet (director of " L'Essor ") and starred Yves Desprey in the rôle of Robert.

In 1942, in Tunis, Gide had assisted " L'Essor " in organizing an " école du théâtre " to prepare its young and inexperienced members for work with the main troupe. When, in 1945, Alexandre Fichet returned to Tunis after deportation by the Gestapo, Gide presented him with *L'Intérêt général* for production the following year (cf. *Gavroche*, 2 mai 1946).

That the play was well received by the Tunisian press and public is apparent from an article by H. Fuseiller: " Vie Intellectuelle," in the *Revue de la Vie Tunisienne* (mai 1946, p. 27):

Les succès mensuels remportés par l'Essor sont depuis plus de trente ans choses si naturelles qu'on ne songerait presque plus à les souligner, si, ce mois-ci, cette remarquable compagnie théâtrale d'amateurs ne s'était particulièrement distinguée en montrant pour la première fois la pièce d'André Gide 'Robert ou l'Intérêt général.' C'est donc d'une création que l'Essor a fait bénéficier le public tunisien, création dont le succès a été tel, tant à cause de la perfection et de l'ingéniosité de la mise en scène que de la magistrale interprétation. . . .

II. NOTES ON THE TRANSLATIONS AND ADAPTATIONS

1. *Antoine et Cléopâtre (1920)*

Gide's prose translation of the Shakespeare play, requested by Ida Rubinstein in 1915, was not begun until April 1917, and was completed by November 22 of the same year. Gide's translation—an abridgement of the original—was first presented by Ida Rubinstein at the Théâtre de l'Opéra on June 14, 1920. Edouard de Max played Antoine and Mme Rubinstein was Cléopâtre. M. Desfontaines directed the *mise en scène, décors* and costumes were by M. Drésa and music by Florent Schmitt.

In the *Journal* for May 11, 1920 (p. 681)—at the time of the rehearsals for the Rubinstein production—Gide complains:

Le monotone débit des acteurs égalise le texte et le ponce. . . . Il ne paraît qu'aucun d'eux soit sensible à la beauté des mots en eux-mêmes. . . . Je me persuade une fois de plus de l'impossibilité de faire d'une pièce de théâtre une oeuvre d'art.

Gide's dissatisfaction with this production would seem to have been shared by the Paris critics:

Fernand Gregh:
. . . la mise èn scène de chaque décor exigeait dix minutes. . . . Le fil de l'action se rompait sans cesse.   —*Comoedia* (15 juin 1920).

Régis Gignoux:
Il n'y a pas à défendre Shakespeare. Il se défend tout seul. M. André Gide l'y eût aidé avec sa traduction, mais pour se permettre de qualifier cette traduction, il faudrait l'avoir entendue. On ne l'entendit pas. . . . Quant à la tragédie, elle garde la coupe de Shakespeare, sauf quelques suppressions. . . .
    —*Le Figaro* (15 juin 1920).

In 1937 Gide undertook the correction and revision of his first translation. His new version of the play was completed by September 1938 and, it seems, to his entire satisfaction. Gide wrote then that his improvements and additions to the original translation "m'ont fait sentir bien défectueuse ma première version; mais je la crois presque excellente à présent." (*Journal*, p. 1319)

8

The enlarged and definitive *Antoine et Cléopâtre* was first presented at the Comédie-Française beginning on April 27, 1945 and continuing through the summer. The production was directed by Jean-Louis Barrault, *décors* were by Jean Hugo and music by Jacques Ibert. Included in the cast were: Marie Bell (Cléopâtre), Aimé Clairond (Antoine), Denis d'Inès (Le Devin), Jean Chevrier (Octave), Louis Seigner (Lépide), Escande (Agrippa), Maurice Donneaud (Sextus Pompée), J.-L. Barrault (Eros), Pierre Dux (Enobarbus).

The following comments are representative of the enthusiastic critical response to the play:

Philippe Hériat:
> Une langue unique, moderne et classique, et qui aborde sans dissonance les verdeurs shakespeariennes, relève à tout instant le dialogue. . . .   —*La Bataille* (3 mai 1945).

François Mauriac:
> La mise en scène de Jean-Louis Barrault, les décors de Jean Hugo pas une seconde ne nous détournent du texte immortel dont le traducteur, André Gide, a pesé chaque terme avec scrupule.
>   —*Opéra* (9 mai 1945).

Léon Moussinac:
> Certainement la création théâtrale la plus riche de cette saison avare. . . . Le sens, le goût et la passion du théâtre.
>   —*Opéra* (9 mai 1945).

2. *Amal et la Lettre du Roi (1928)*

Gide's translation of Rabindranath Tagore's *Post-Office* dates from 1914. Copeau had intended presenting *Amal* at the Vieux Colombier but his retirement prevented this realization. Gide then entrusted his translation to "La Petite Scène" which gave the first presentation of *Amal* on May 16, 1928. (No mention is made of this production in the *notices* of the *Théâtre complet–IV–*or in the theatre section of the Naville *Bibliographie*.) *Mise en scène* and *décor* were by Xavier de Courville (director of the "Petite Scène") and the main rôles were played by Yves Bourdier (Amal) and Henry de Longrais (Madhav).

The reaction of the Paris press to this 1928 production was generally enthusiastic:

Gerard d'Houville:
> Rien de plus délicatement mélancolique que ces deux actes si bien traduits par André Gide.
>   —*Le Figaro* (28 mai 1928).

Franc-Nohain:
> Il faut savoir gré à M. André Gide de nous avoir fait connaître, en
> la traduisant avec cette ferveur, cette habileté et cette élégance, la
> mélancolique et poétique comédie de Rabindranath Tagore.
> <div align="right">—<i>Echo</i> (19 mai 1928).</div>

During its 1936-37 season the Compagnie George Pitoëff presented *Amal* at the Théâtre des Mathurins. With *mise en scène* and
décor by Pitoëff and music by Darius Milhaud, the production was
noteworthy for Ludmilla Pitoëff's performance as Amal.

As part of a "Hommage à André Gide," the play was presented
by the Rideau de Paris beginning June 15, 1949, at the Théâtre
des Mathurins. (Gide's *Enfant prodigue* completed the program.)
Jean Marchat directed this production, *décor* was by Michel Juncar
and music by Louis Martin. Muni played the rôle of Amal with
Charles Nissar as Madhav and Marchat as Gaffer.

3. *Les Caves du Vatican—adaptation by Yvonne Lartigaud (1933).*

On October 24, 1933, *Les Caves du Vatican*, "sotie en 9 jeux,"
adapted from the Gide work by Yvonne Lartigaud, was presented
by the group "Art et Travail" at the Studio des Champs-Elysées.
The production was directed by Firmin Gémier with *décors* and
costumes by Akakia Viala. Principals in the cast were: Marc
Darnault (Lafcadio), Edmond Lartigaud (Julius), Hélène Lerou-
ville (Comtesse de Saint-Prix), Guy Favières (Fleurissoire) and
Harry Krimer (Protos).

In an interview in *Paris-Midi* (24 oct. 1933) Gide remarked:
"Je ne pense pas qu'on eût pu tirer des dialogues de mon livre
un meilleur parti." But he adds:

Eussé-je fait une pièce du sujet des *Caves du Vatican*, je l'aurais écrite
tout différemment et me serais en particuliar préoccupé de resserrer une
intrigue qui, sur la scène, a quelque mal à se nouer.

It indeed seems strange that Gémier's troupe, "Art et Travail"
—dedicated to an "art théâtral populaire"—should have chosen
this rather complicated adaptation of Gide's diffuse and philosophic
sotie for its initial presentation. As for the critics, they found little
to praise in this production:

James de Coquet:
> Cette nouvelle compagnie . . . veut faire du théâtre 'qui ait un

sens social et humain.' . . . Mais il faut bien reconnaître que M. André Gide n'est pas l'auteur populaire par excellence. . . .

—*Le Figaro* (28 oct. 1933).

Pierre Brisson:

Le livre de M. Gide, un des plus diffus qu'il ait écrits, n'incitaient guère à une transposition théâtrale. L'esprit en devient méconnaissable. . . .

—*Le Temps* (30 oct. 1933)

Gérard Bauer:

Nos pères avaient raison: M. André Gide n'était pas fait pour le théâtre, et sauf quelques scènes de *Saül* et d'*Antoine et Cléopâtre* (qui valent mieux d'être lues encore par un Jacques Copeau que d'être jouées), ses oeuvres dramatiques sont aussi peu scéniques qu'on peut l'être.

—*Annales* (3 nov. 1933).

4. *Les Caves du Vatican—adaptation by André Gide (1933).*

Despite the poor reception given the Lartigaud adaptation, Gide completed in 1933 a three-act dramatization of his *Caves du Vatican* (cf. *T. C.*, V). Gide's play—a more faithful and ordered representation of the original than was Mme Lartigaud's succession of burlesque "jeux" and "guignolesque" caricatures—was first presented by the Société Belles-Lettres at Montreux on December 9, 1933, then at Lausanne on December 15, and finally at Geneva on December 18.

While not attaching great significance to this Swiss production of his play, the *Journal* entries for Nov.-Dec. 1933 show Gide to be genuinely interested in the work of the Bellettriens and not at all dissatisfied with the results.

Lausanne, 30 nov. 1933:

Installé ici depuis trois semaines, je surveille et fais semblant de diriger les répétitions de . . . mes *Caves du Vatican*, que les jeunes Bellettriens lausannois se sont mis en tête de représenter pour leur fête annuelle. Excellente occasion de prendre contact avec la jeunesse de la Suisse romande. (p. 1188)

Genève, 14 déc. 1933:

. . . la scène, sensiblement plus petite que celle de Lausanne, s'est mieux laissé animer par des acteurs qui, au surplus, savaient mieux leurs rôles. La bonne volonté du public églait, surpassait même celle du public de Montreux. (p. 1190)

A revised version of Gide's original adaptation—in two acts and seventeen tableaux—had its *première* at the Comédie-Françise on

December 13, 1950. Jean Meyer directed the production and the cast included: Roland Alexandre (Lafcadio), Henri Rollan (Julius), Renée Faure (Geneviève), Georges Chamarat (Fleurissoire) and Jean Meyer (Protos). Most critics found the play mechanical and uninspiring.

Jean-Jacques Gautier:

> Tout le comique, toute l'énorme cocasserie de l'ouvrage a disparu. . . . Le mystère s'est volatisé aux feux de la rampe, et l'atmosphère rocambolesque d'un grand nombre d'épisodes s'est trouvé ramenée au climat d'un solennel exercice de marionnettes.
>
> —*Le Figaro* (18 déc. 1950).

Robert Kemp:

> . . . Déception que le roman ne donnait pas; ou donnait moins. Mais le théâtre exige tant de vigueur. Le dessin au trait, les crayons menus des *Caves*, font de la satire et des hardiesses philosophiques où visait M. Gide de la satire de petite gazette, de la philosophie de boîte à joujoux.   —*Le Monde* (17, 18 déc. 1950).

5. *Hamlet (1946)*

An important event of the 1946-47 theatrical season (which included the Hamlets of Marcel Pagnol, Michel Arnaud and the Shakespeare original) was the Jean-Louis Barrault production of the Gide translation of *Hamlet*, first presented at the Théâtre Marigny on October 17, 1946. With *mise en scène* by Barrault, *décors* by Henri Masson and music by Arthur Honegger, the cast included: J.-L. Barrault (Hamlet), Jacqueline Bouvier (Ophélie), Marie-Hélène Dasté (La Reine), Pierre Renoir (Le Roi), Jean Desailly (Horatius), André Brunot (Polonius) and Roger Rudel (Laertes). *Hamlet* has since remained on the Marigny repertory.

Gide had started translating *Hamlet* as early as 1922 but, after completing the first act, had abandoned the project. A meeting with Barrault on May 4, 1942, at Marseilles, encouraged him to continue the play during his subsequent stay in Tunisia. Where, by Gide's admission, the original first act had required more time and effort than the entire five acts of *Antoine et Cléopâtre*, he was now able to complete the remaining four acts of *Hamlet* in just three months of concentrated effort. It was at Sidi bou Saïd, on August 30, 1942, that the work was finished.

Gide's "lettre non-envoyée à André Thérive," dated 14 mai

1928 (*O. C.*, XV, 541 ff.), enlightens us as to his views on translations and translators:

Un bon traducteur doit bien savoir la langue de l'auteur qu'il traduit, mais mieux encore la sienne propre, et j'entends par là: non seulement être capable de l'écrire correctement, mais en connaître les substilités, les souplesses, les ressources cachées. . . .

. . . Les versions [de mes prédécesseurs] souvent très exactes, avaient le défaut de rester livresques, c'est-à-dire parfaitement impropres à la scène, et défaut beaucoup plus grave à mes yeux, s'attachant de trop près à la lettre, de négliger certaines qualités poétiques. . . .

Je crois absurde de se cramponner au texte de trop près . . . ce n'est pas seulement le sens qu'il s'agit de rendre; il importe de ne pas traduire des mots, mais des phrases, et d'exprimer, sans rien perdre, pensée et émotion. . . .

(Cf., also, for Gide's views as translator, his interview with Philip Roddman: "Gide's Hamlet," *Partisan Review*, XVI (Feb. 1949), pp. 213-220.)

Typical of the press reaction to Barrault's production were:

Jean-Jacques Gautier:
> Il ne lui était pas possible . . . de disposer d'un texte plus simple, mieux adapté, plus coulant, mieux traduit, moins traître et plus théâtral que celui de M. André Gide.
>> —*Le Figaro* (18 oct. 1946).

René Bizet:
> . . . La force concentrée . . . les nets raccourcis, la poésie qui 'tord son cou' à l'éloquence . . . ce choix judicieux des mots, cette fermeté de la phrase sont particulièrement sensibles à l'oreille.
>> —*Paris-Presse* (19 oct. 1946).

Gabriel Marcel:
> . . . M. Barrault est un Hamlet extraordinaire—le plus grand sans doute qu'on ait vu en France depuis Mounet-Sully.
>> —*Les Nouvelles Littéraires* (24 oct. 1946).

6. *Le Procès (1947)*

The Gide-Barrault adaptation of Kafka's novel—based on the French translation of Alexandre Vialette—was first presented by the Compagnie Madeleine Renaud—J.-L. Barrault on October 10, 1947, at the Théâtre Marigny. *Mise en scène* was by Barrault and *décors* and costumes by Félix Labisse. Barrault played the rôle of Joseph K. and Madeleine Renaud was Léni. *Le Procès* has since remained on the Marigny repertory.

In a *Journal* entry for 1940, Gide writes of his great admiration for the Kafka novel, and adds: " L'angoisse que ce livre respire est, par moments, presque intolérable ; car comment ne pas se dire: cet être traqué, c'est moi? " (*Journal '39-'42*, p. 70). But, as in the case of *Hamlet*, it was the intervention of Jean-Louis Barrault (again, at their Marseilles meeting of May 4, 1942) that brought the stage adaptation of *Le Procès* to fruition. In a revealing interview in *Le Monde* (2 oct. 1947), Gide speaks of Barrault's enthusiasm for their project. To Gide, the difficulties of such an adaptation seemed at first insurmountable, but Barrault's insistence won the day:

A mon retour en France, en 1945, il revint à la charge. Il avait travaillé de son côté et me remit un scénario déjà détaillé. . . . Il ne s'agissait plus que de couvrir de chair le squelette qu'il m'apportait, ce que je fis avec enthousiasme. Au surplus, m'effaçant le plus possible pour céder la place à Kafka, je me servis autant que je le pouvais de l'excellente traduction de Vialette. . . . Si cette traduction hardie remporte le succès que je crois qu'elle mérite (car je la tiens pour extraordinaire dans sa forme, sa présentation, sa portée) c'est à Jean-Louis Barrault surtout, comme initiateur et réalisateur aussi bien que comme interprète, qu'en devra revenir l'honneur.

A cross-section of the generally favorable press commentary follows:

Paul Claudel:
> Magnifique spectacle! Exemple inouï, dans l'art du comédien, d'une espèce d'héroïsme surhumain!
> —*Le Figaro Littéraire* (18 oct. 1947).

Thierry-Maulnier:
> Curieuse rencontre que celle qui se fait, sur les planches, entre un roman qui est à peine un roman, mais plutôt une confession ' existentielle ' et une parabole métaphysique, et un mode d'expression théâtral qui est à peine du théâtre, mais plutôt de la danse.
> —*Le Spectateur* (21 oct. 1947).

Jean H. Roy:
> La réussite est . . . incontestable et d'autant plus méritoire que la difficulté était grande.
> —*Les Temps Modernes* (no. 29, fév. 1948, p. 1535).

7. Miscellaneous

(i) *Le Prométhée mal enchaîné* (1928)—" sotie en un prologue et trois actes," produced and directed by Renée and Arnold Naville, 1928.

(ii) *Jardin public* (1934)—a ballet, taken from an episode of Gide's *Faux-Monnayeurs* and presented at the Théâtre des Champs-Elysées, May-June 1934, by the Ballets Russes de Monte-Carlo. Music was by Vladimir Dukelsky, choreography by Léonide Massine and David Lichine with *décor* and costumes by Jean Lurcat.

(iii) *Arden de Feversham* (1937)—Gide's translation of the English play, given a "représentation partielle" in 1937 by the Rideau de Paris at the Comédie des Champs-Elysées. *Mise en scène* by Marcel Herrand.

BIBLIOGRAPHY

1. GIDE EDITIONS CONSULTED:

Oeuvres complètes d'André Gide, 15 vol., Paris, Gallimard, 1932-1939.
Théâtre complet, 8 vol., Neuchâtel et Paris, Ides et Calendes, 1947-1949.

Un Esprit non prévenu, Paris, Kra, 1929.
L'Ecole des femmes, suivi de *Robert*, Paris, Gallimard, 1930.
Lettres, Liège, A la Lampe d'Aladdin, 1930.
La Séquestrée de Poitiers, Paris, Gallimard, 1930.
Geneviève, Paris, Gallimard, 1936.
Retour de l'U. R. S. S., Paris, Gallimard, 1936.
Retouches à mon Retour de l'U. R. S. S., Paris, Gallimard, 1937.
Découvrons Henri Michaux, Paris, Gallimard, 1941.
Interviews imaginaires. La Délivrance de Tunis, New York, Jacques Schiffrin, 1943.
Attendu que . . ., Alger, Charlot, 1943.
Pages de Journal, 1939-1942, New York, Jacques Schiffrin, 1944.
Thésée, New York, Jacques Schiffrin, 1946.
Le Retour, Neuchâtel et Paris, Ides et Calendes, 1946.
Poétique, Neuchâtel et Paris, Ides et Calendes, 1946.
Journal, 1899-1939, 4th edit., Paris, Gallimard, 1948.
Correspondance, 1893-1938, F. Jammes, A. Gide, Paris, Gallimard, 1948.
Préfaces, Neuchâtel et Paris, Ides et Calendes, 1948.
Rencontres, Neuchâtel et Paris, Ides et Calendes, 1948.
Eloges, Neuchâtel et Paris, Ides et Calendes, 1948.
Feuillets d'Automne, Paris, Mercure de France, 1949.
Anthologie de la poésie française, Paris, Gallimard, 1949.
Correspondance, 1899-1926, P. Claudel, A. Gide, Paris, Gallimard, 1949.
Journal, 1942-1949, Paris, Gallimard, 1950.
Littérature engagée, Paris, Gallimard, 1950.
Et nunc manet in te, suivi de Journal intime, Neuchâtel et Paris, Ides et Calendes, 1951.
Ainsi soit-il, ou les Jeux sont faits, Paris, Gallimard, 1952.

2. CRITICAL AND BIBLIOGRAPHICAL

Alibert, F.-P., *En Marge d'André Gide*, Paris, Oeuvres Representatives, 1930.

111

112   THE THEATRE OF ANDRÉ GIDE

Ames, Van Meter, *André Gide*, Norfolk, New Directions, 1947.
Archambault, Paul, *Humanité d'André Gide*, Paris, Bloud et Gay, 1946.
Bernstein, Henry, et al., *Hommage à André Gide*, Paris, Edit. du Capitole, 1928.
Braak, Sybrandi, *André Gide et l'Ame moderne*, Amsterdam, H. J. Paris, 1923.
Davet, Yvonne, *Autour des Nourritures terrestres*, Paris, Gallimard, 1948.
Drain, Henri, *Nietzsche et Gide*, Paris, Edit. de la Madeleine, 1932.
Du Bos, Charles, *Le Dialogue avec André Gide*, Paris, Au Sans Pareil, 1929.
Fayer, Mischa Harry, *Gide, Freedom and Dostoyevsky*, Burlington, Vt., Lane Press, 1946.
Fernandez, Ramon, *André Gide*, Paris, Corrêa, 1931.
——, et al., *André Gide et notre temps*, Paris, Gallimard, 1935.
Gabory, Georges, *André Gide: Son Oeuvre*, Paris, Edit. de la Nouv. Revue Critique, 1924.
Gouiran, Emile, *André Gide: Essai de psychologie littéraire*, Paris, Jean Crès, 1934.
Hytier, Jean, *André Gide*, Alger, Charlot, 1938.
Iseler, Paul, *Les Débuts d'André Gide vus par Pierre Louÿs*, Paris, Edit. du Sagittaire, 1937.
Jean-Aubry, G., *André Gide et la musique*, Paris, Edit. de la Revue Musicale, 1945.
Lalou, René, *André Gide*, Strasbourg, Joseph Heissler, 1928.
Lang, Renée, *André Gide et la pensée allemande*, Paris, Edit. Luf, 1949.
Larbaud, Valéry, *Lettres à André Gide*, Paris et La Haye, A. A. M. Stols, 1948.
Lepoutre, Raymond, *André Gide*, Paris, Richard-Masse, 1946.
Mann, Klauss, *André Gide: The Crisis of Modern Thought*, New York, Creative Age Press, 1943.
Martinet, Edouard, *André Gide: l'Amour et la divinité*, Paris, Victor Attinger, 1931.
Massis, Henri, *D'André Gide à Marcel Proust*, Lyon, H. Lardanchet, 1948.
Mondor, Henri, *Les Premiers Temps d'une amitié: André Gide et Paul Valéry*, Monaco, Edit. du Rocher, 1947.
Naville, Arnold, *Bibliographie des écrits de André Gide*, Paris, H. Matarasso, 1949.
Naville, Claude, *André Gide et le communisme*, Paris, Lib. du Travail, 1936.
Nobécourt, R.-G., *Les Nourritures normandes d'André Gide*, Paris, Edit. Médicis, 1949.
O'Brien, Justin, tr., intro. and notes: *The Journals of André Gide*, 3 vol., New York, Knopf, 1947-1949.
——, et ses élèves à Columbia Univ., " Index détaillé des quinze volumes de l'édition Gallimard des *Oeuvres complètes d'André Gide*," New York, 1949 (mimeo.).

Pell, Elsie, *André Gide: l'Evolution de sa pensée religieuse*, Paris, Henri
    Didier, 1936.
Pierre-Quint, Léon, *André Gide, sa vie, son oeuvre*, Paris, Stock, 1932.
Poucel, Victor, *L'Esprit d'André Gide*, Paris, à l'Art Catholique, 1929.
Rivière, Jacques, *Etudes*, 12th edit., Paris, Gallimard, 1936.
Rouveyre, André, *Le Reclus et le Retors: Gourmont et Gide*, Paris, Crès,
    1927.
Schwob, René, *Le Vrai Drame d'André Gide*, Paris, B. Grasset, 1932.
Souday, Paul, *André Gide*, Paris, Kra, 1927.

3. GENERAL REFERENCE

Bentley, Eric, *The Playwright as Thinker*, New York, Reynal and Hitchcock,
    1946.
Bergson, Henri, *Le Rire, essai sur la signification du comique*, Paris, Félix
    Alcan, 1912.
Bray, René, *La Formation de la doctrine classique en France*, Paris,
    Hachette, 1927.
Brisson, Pierre, *Le Théâtre des années folles* (1919-1940), Genève, Edit. du
    Milieu du Monde, 1943.
Chase, Richard, *Quest for Myth*, Baton Rouge, Louisiana State Univ.
    Press, 1949.
Claudel, Paul, *Positions et propositions*, 9th edit., Paris, Gallimard, 1928.
Clouard, Henri, *Histoire de la littérature francaise du symbolisme à nos
    jours*, 2 vol., Paris, Albin Michel, 1947-1949.
Coindreau, Maurice, *La Farce est jouée: vingt-cinq ans de théâtre français*
    (1900-1925), New York, Edit. de la Maison Française, 1942.
Copeau, Jacques, *Critiques d'un autre Temps*, 9th edit., Paris, Gallimard,
    1923.
Freud, Sigmund, *Basic Writings*, tr. and ed. by A. A. Brill, New York,
    Random House, 1938.
Gouhier, Henri, *Essence du Théâtre*, Paris, Plon, 1943.
Hebbel, Friedrich, *Three Plays*, tr. by L. H. Allen et al., London, J. M.
    Dent and Sons, 1914.
Herodotus, *History*, 4 vol., tr. by George Rawlinson, London, John Murray,
    1862.
Highet, Gilbert, *The Classical Tradition*, New York, Oxford Univ. Press,
    1949.
Kemp, Robert, *Lectures dramatiques*, Paris, Edit. Marcel Daubin, 1947.
Knowles, Dorothy, *La Réaction idéaliste au théâtre depuis 1890*, Paris,
    Droz, 1934.
Loiseau, Hippolyte, *Goethe et la France*, Paris, Victor Attinger, 1930.
Morino, Lina, *La NRF dans l'histoire des lettres*, Paris, Gallimard, 1939.
Norwood, Gilbert, *Greek Tragedy*, London, Methuen and Co., 1920.
Pillement, Georges, *Anthologie du théâtre français contemporain*, 3 vol.,
    Paris, Edit. du Bélier, 1945-1948.
Raymond, Marcel, *Le Jeu retrouvé*, Montreal, Edit. de l'Arbre, 1943.

Ross, Flora Emma, *Goethe in Modern France*, Urbana, Univ. of Illinois (Studies in Lang. and Lit., XXI), 1937.

Sophocles, tr. of his plays by F. Storr, 2 vol., London, Wm. Heinemann, 1924 (I), 1939 (II).

Stendhal, *Mélanges de littérature*, 3 vol., Paris, Le Divan, 1933.

Touchard, Pierre-Aimé, *Dyonisos, apologie pour le théâtre d'Eschyle à Paul Claudel*, Paris, Edit. du Seuil, 1949.

Wilson, Edmund, *Axel's Castle*, New York, Charles Scribner, 1936.

Worcester, David, *The Art of Satire*, Cambridge, Harvard Univ. Press, 1940.

4. PERIODICAL REFERENCES IN MAIN TEXT

Gide, André, " Faits-Divers," *Nouvelle Revue Française*, XXX (juin 1928), pp. 829-849.

———, " Goethe," *Nouvelle Revue Française*, XXXVIII (mars 1932), pp. 368-377.

———, " Lettres à Christian Beck," *Mercure de France*, CCCVI (août 1949), pp. 616-637.

Jaloux, Edmond, " André Gide," *La Revue Hebdomadaire* (16 janvier 1932), pp. 267-286.

Louverné, Jean, " Conversion?," *Nouvelle Revue Française*, XLII (avril 1934), pp. 628-648.

Thibaudet, Albert, " Conversions et Conclusions," *Nouvelle Revue Française*, XLII (juin 1934), pp. 997-1003.

INDEX OF PERSONS